ZIG AND WIKKI

in

THE COW

Hey! Come look at this little guy!
Pay attention to ME, Zig!

A TOON BOOK BY

NADJA SPIEGELMAN & TRADE LOEFFLER

For Dash *–Nadja*
For Annalisa, Clark, and Boo *–Trade*

Editorial Director: FRANÇOISE MOULY

Book Design: FRANÇOISE MOULY & JONATHAN BENNETT

Guest Editor: GEOFFREY HAYES

Wikki's Screen Drawings: MYKEN BOMBERGER

TRADE LOEFFLER'S artwork was drawn in black ink on paper and colored digitally

A TOON Book™ © 2009 RAW Junior, LLC, 27 Greene Street, New York, NY 10013. TOON Books®, TOON Graphics™, LITTLE LIT® and TOON Into Reading™ are trademarks of RAW Junior, LLC. All rights reserved. No part of this book may be used or reproduced in any manner whatsoever without written permission except in the case of brief quotations embodied in critical articles and reviews. All our books are Smyth Sewn (the highest library-quality binding available) and printed with soy-based inks on acid-free woodfree paper harvested from responsible sources. All photos used by permission. Page 8: © Igor Burchenkov / iStockphoto.com; Page 16: © 2011 Kyle Slade; Page 19: © Zralok / Dreamstime.com; Page 20: © Shariffc / Dreamstime.com; Page 21: © Vlue / Dreamstime.com; Page 33: Slides © Mel Yokoyama; Page 40: Cow mouth © 2011 Keven Law (http://www.flickr.com/photos/kevenlaw/), Cow tongue © Kurt / Dreamstime.com, Cow nose © 2011 Jessica Warren; Back cover: Cow © Tilo / Dreamstime.com. Printed in Dongguan, China, by Toppan Leefung. Distributed to the trade by Consortium Book Sales and Distribution, Inc.; orders (800) 283-3572; orderentry@perseusbooks.com; www.cbsd.com.

The Library of Congress has cataloged the hardcover edition as follows:

Spiegelman, Nadja.

Zig and Wikki in The cow : a TOON book / by Nadja Spiegelman & [illustrated by] Trade Loeffler.

    p. cm.

Summary: Two extraterrestrial friends land on Earth in the center of a farm ecosystem, where an argument forces them to separate, only to be brought back together in the stomach of a cow.

ISBN 978-1-935179-15-3 (hardcover)

1. Graphic novels. [1. Graphic novels. 2. Extraterrestrial beings--Fiction. 3. Farms--Fiction. 4. Flies--Fiction.] I. Loeffler, Trade, ill. II. Title. III. Title: Cow.

PZ7.7.S65Zi 2012   741.5'973--dc23   2011026676

ISBN: 978-1-935179-15-3 (hardcover)   ISBN: 978-1-943145-25-6 (paperback)

17 18 19 20 21 22 TPN 10 9 8 7 6 5 4 3 2 1

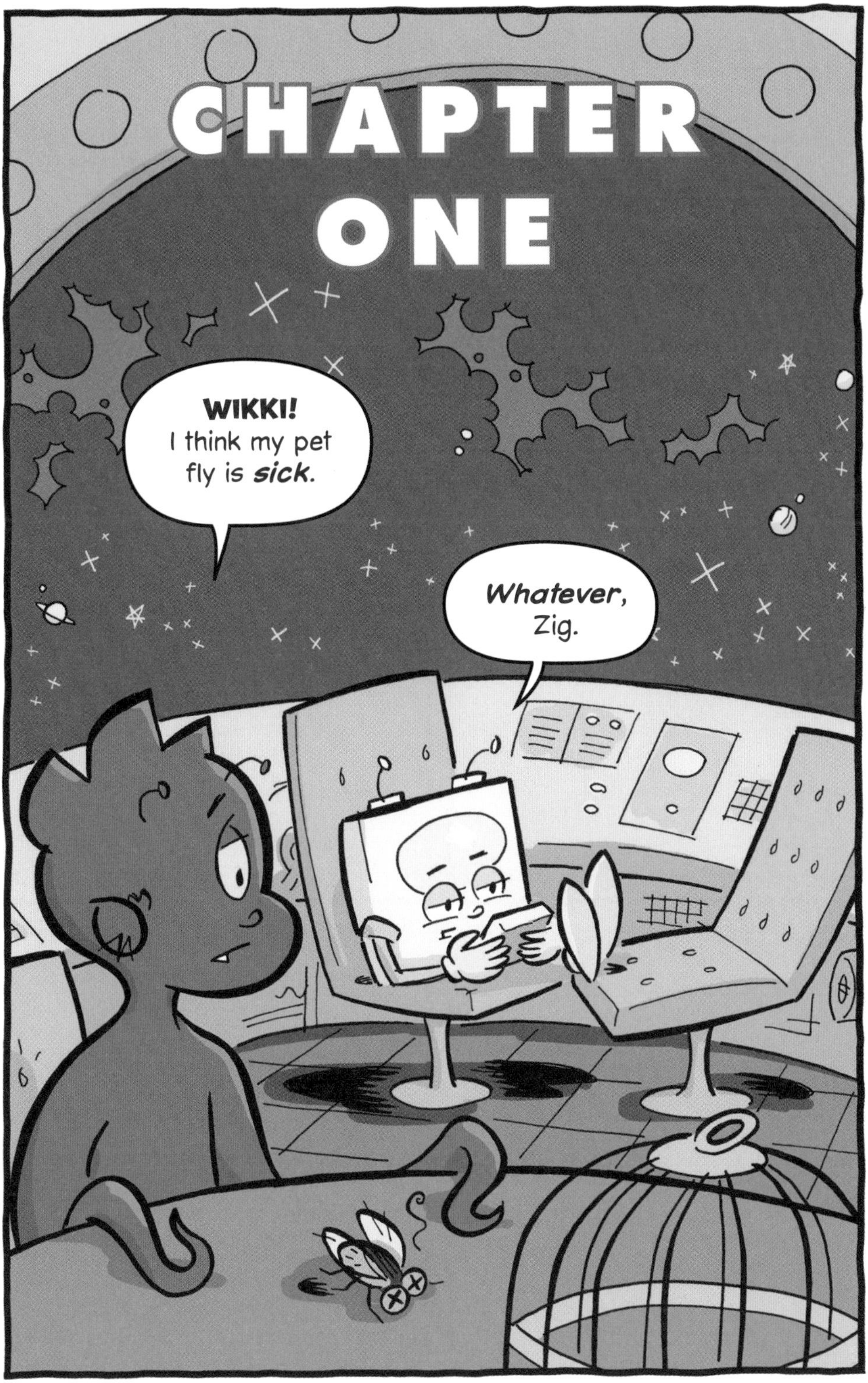
CHAPTER ONE
WIKKI! I think my pet fly is ***sick.***
Whatever, Zig.

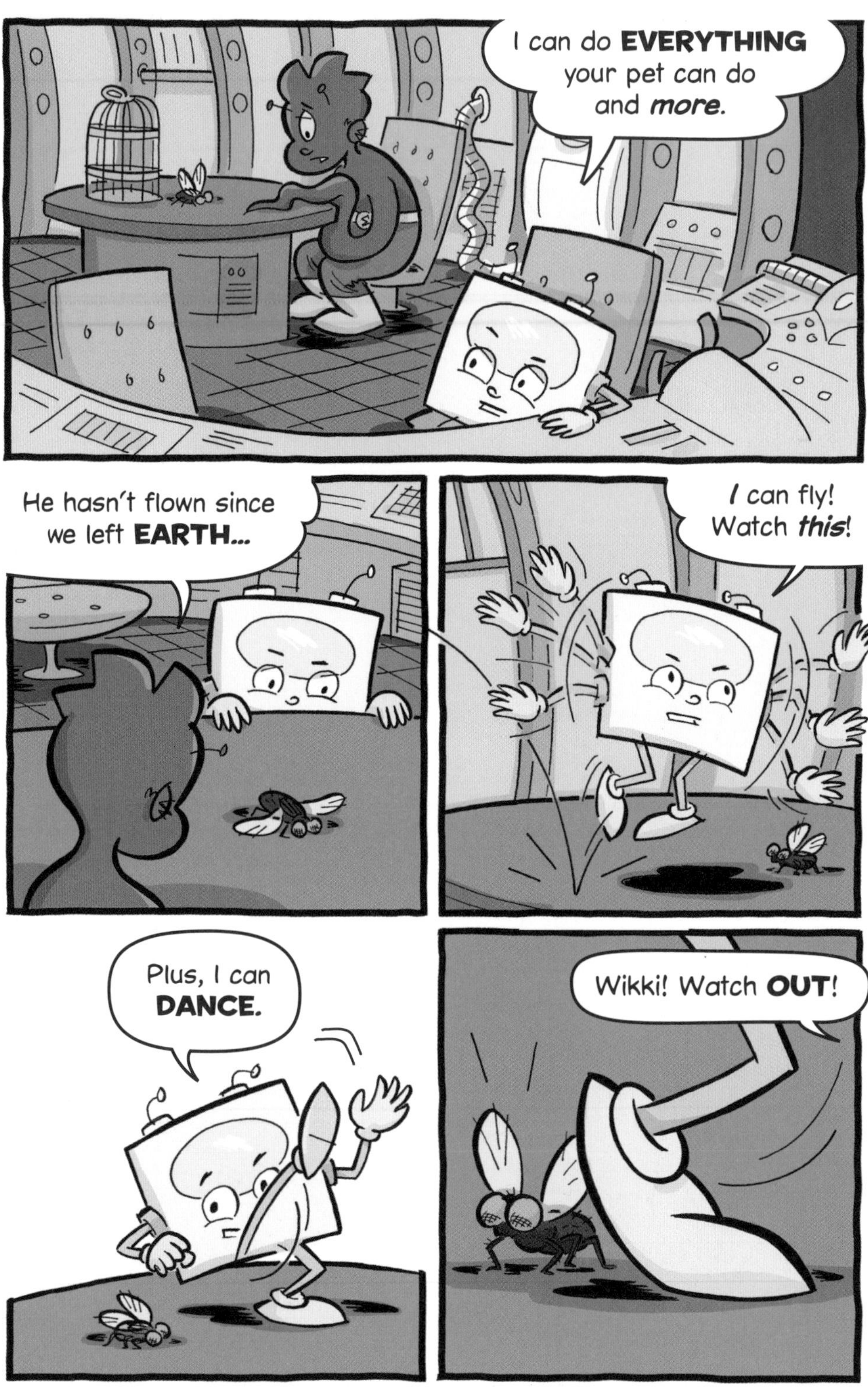
I can do **EVERYTHING** your pet can do and ***more***.
He hasn't flown since we left **EARTH...**
I can fly! Watch ***this***!
Plus, I can **DANCE**.
Wikki! Watch **OUT**!

You almost hurt my **PET**!

You should tell *him* to watch out.

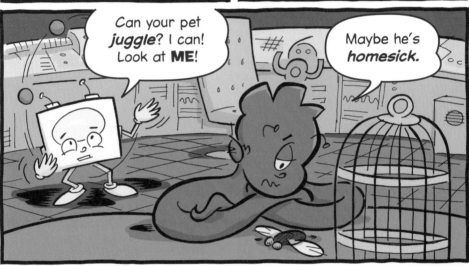

Can your pet *juggle*? I can! Look at **ME**!

Maybe he's *homesick.*

Maybe he's **LAZY**.

Wikki! Your screen is lighting up!

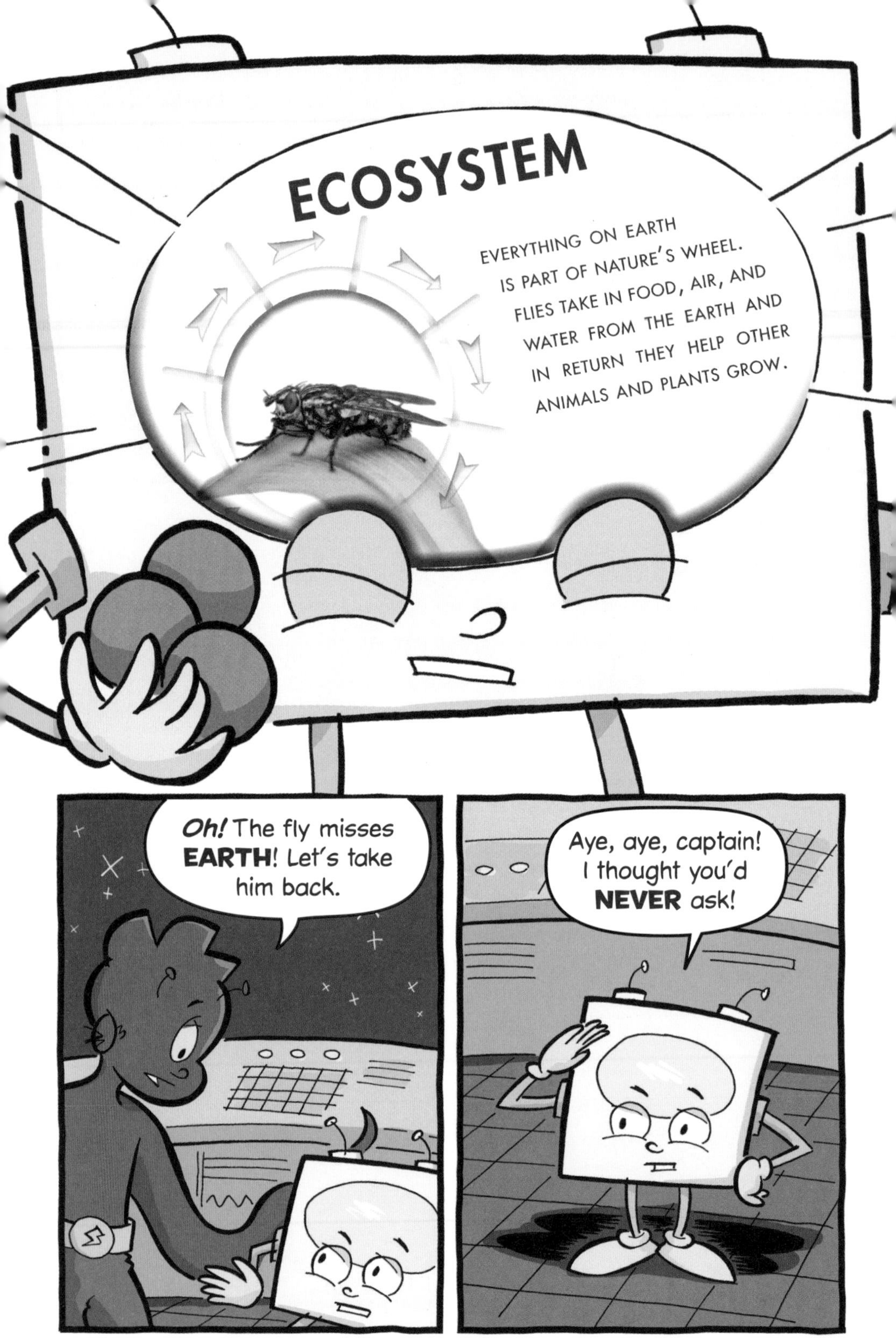
ECOSYSTEM
EVERYTHING ON EARTH IS PART OF NATURE'S WHEEL. FLIES TAKE IN FOOD, AIR, AND WATER FROM THE EARTH AND IN RETURN THEY HELP OTHER ANIMALS AND PLANTS GROW.
Oh! The fly misses **EARTH**! Let's take him back.
Aye, aye, captain! I thought you'd **NEVER** ask!

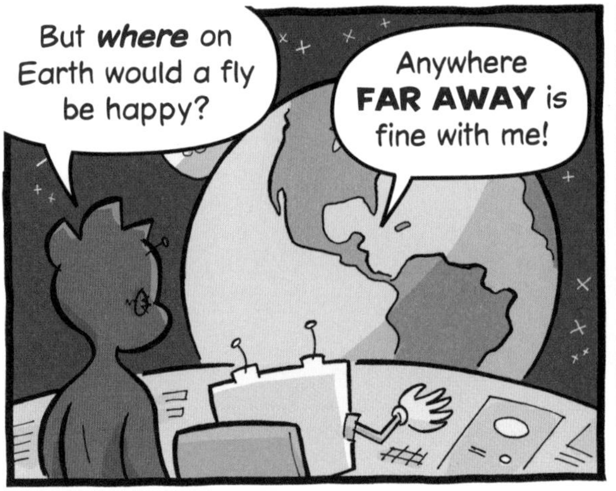
But where on Earth would a fly be happy?
Anywhere FAR AWAY is fine with me!

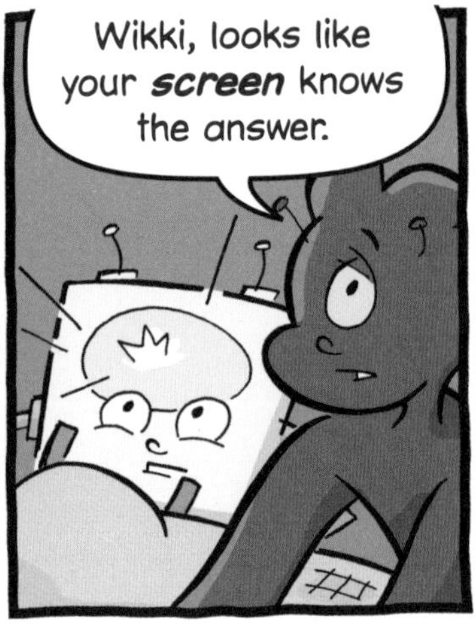
Wikki, looks like your screen knows the answer.

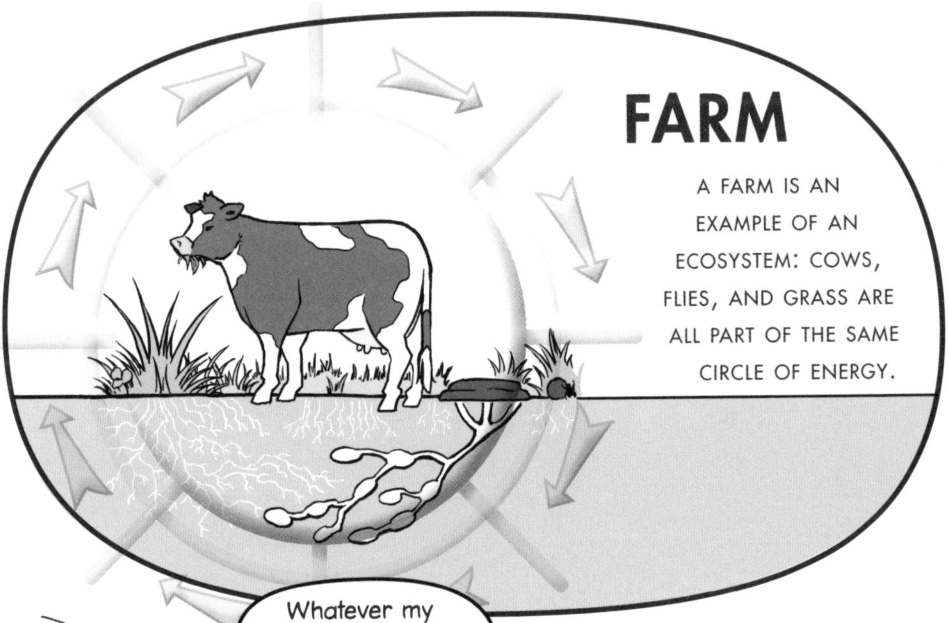
FARM
A FARM IS AN EXAMPLE OF AN ECOSYSTEM: COWS, FLIES, AND GRASS ARE ALL PART OF THE SAME CIRCLE OF ENERGY.

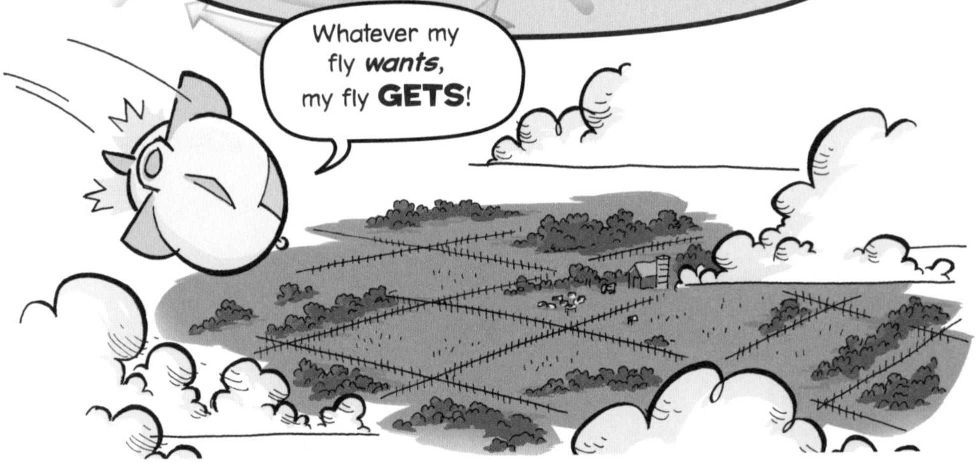
Whatever my fly wants, my fly GETS!

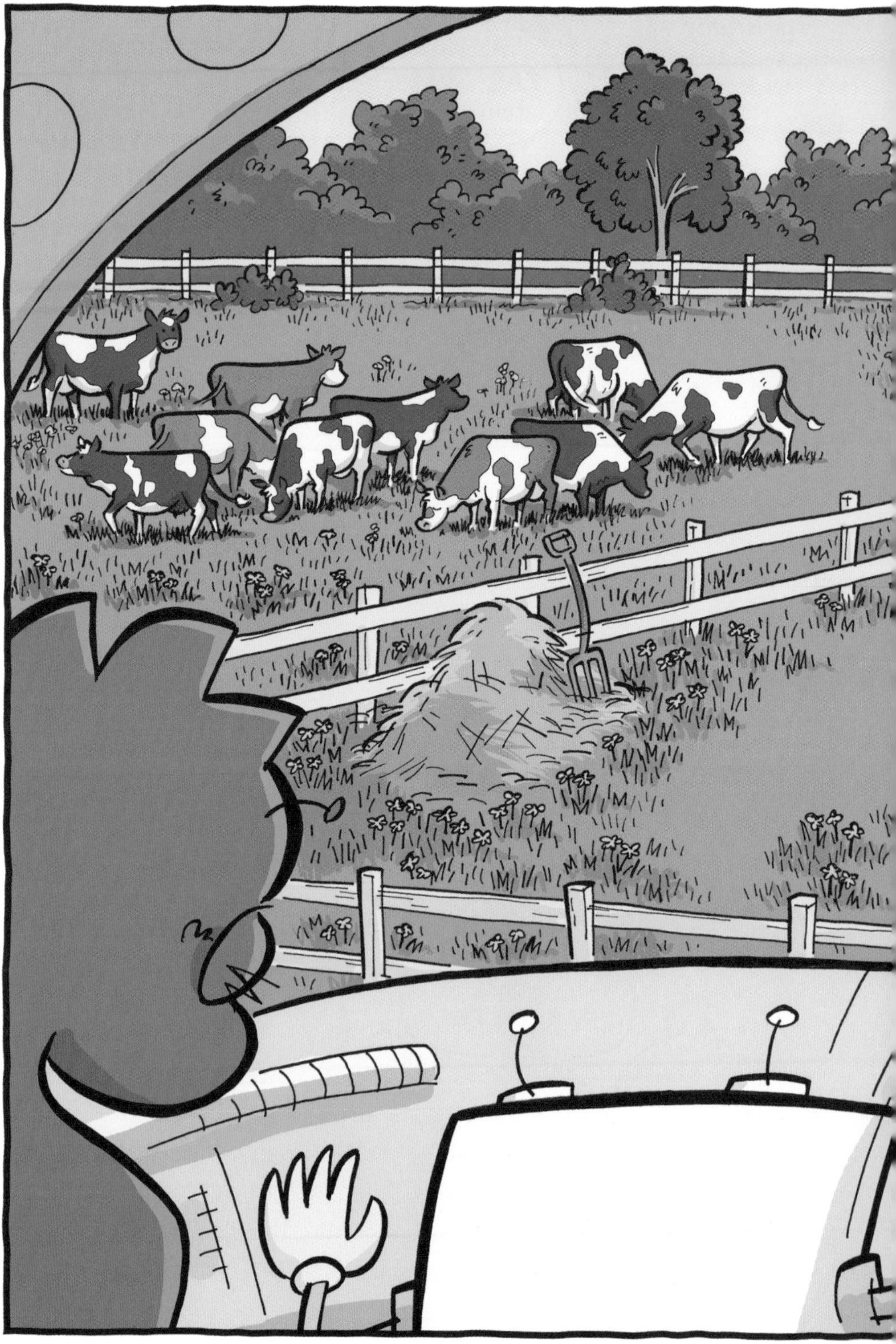

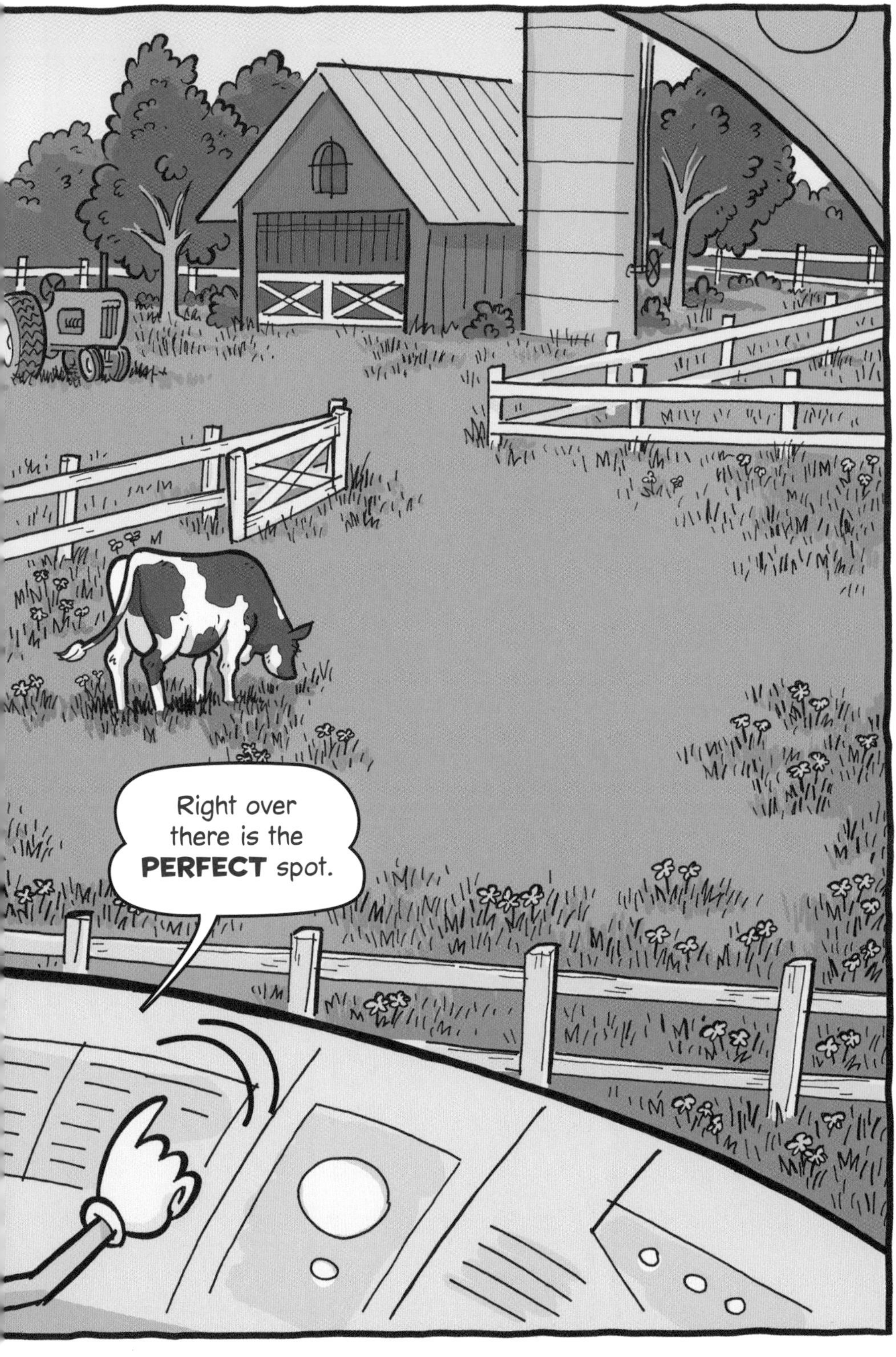
Right over there is the **PERFECT** spot.

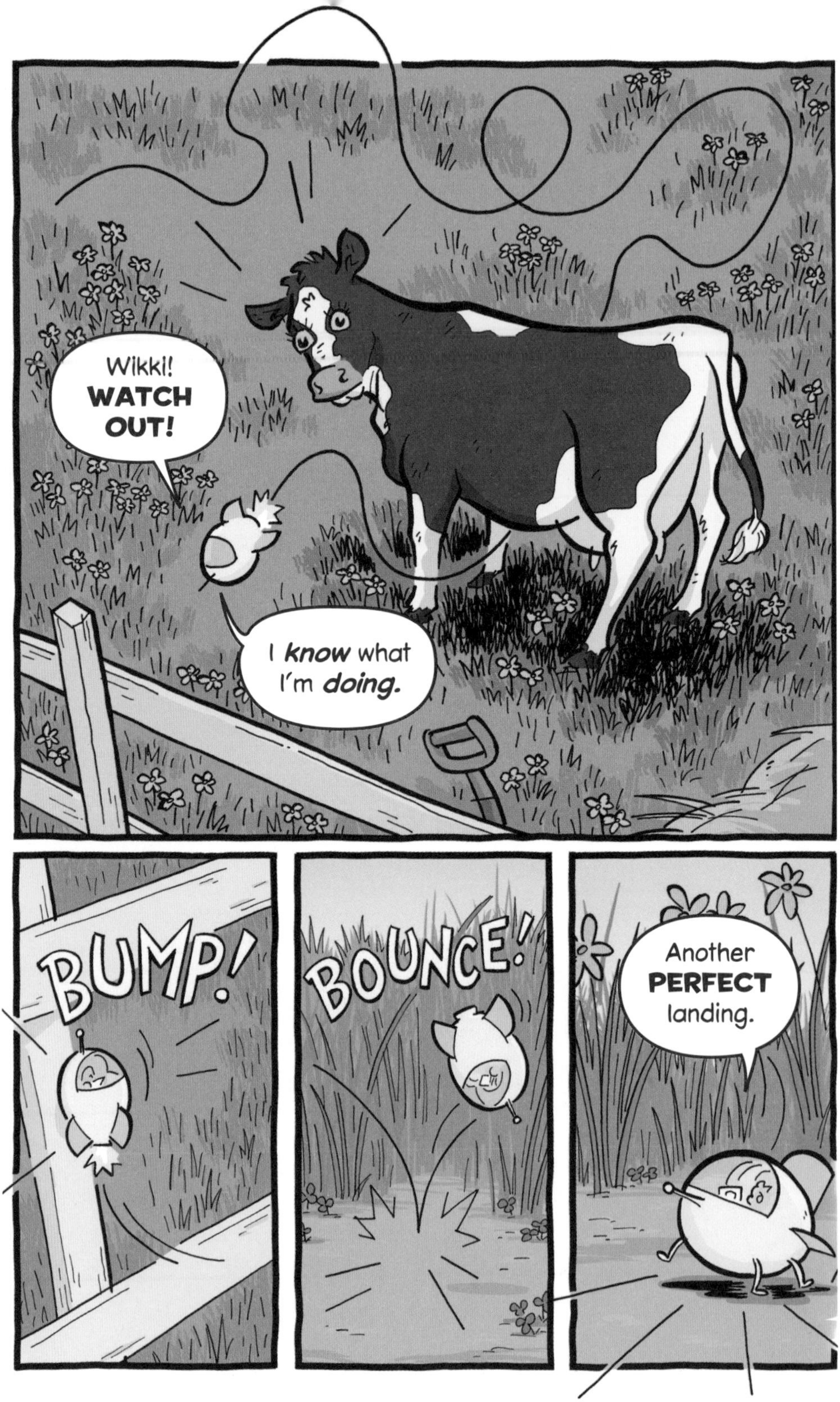
Wikki! **WATCH OUT!**
I ***know*** what I'm ***doing.***
BUMP!
BOUNCE!
Another **PERFECT** landing.

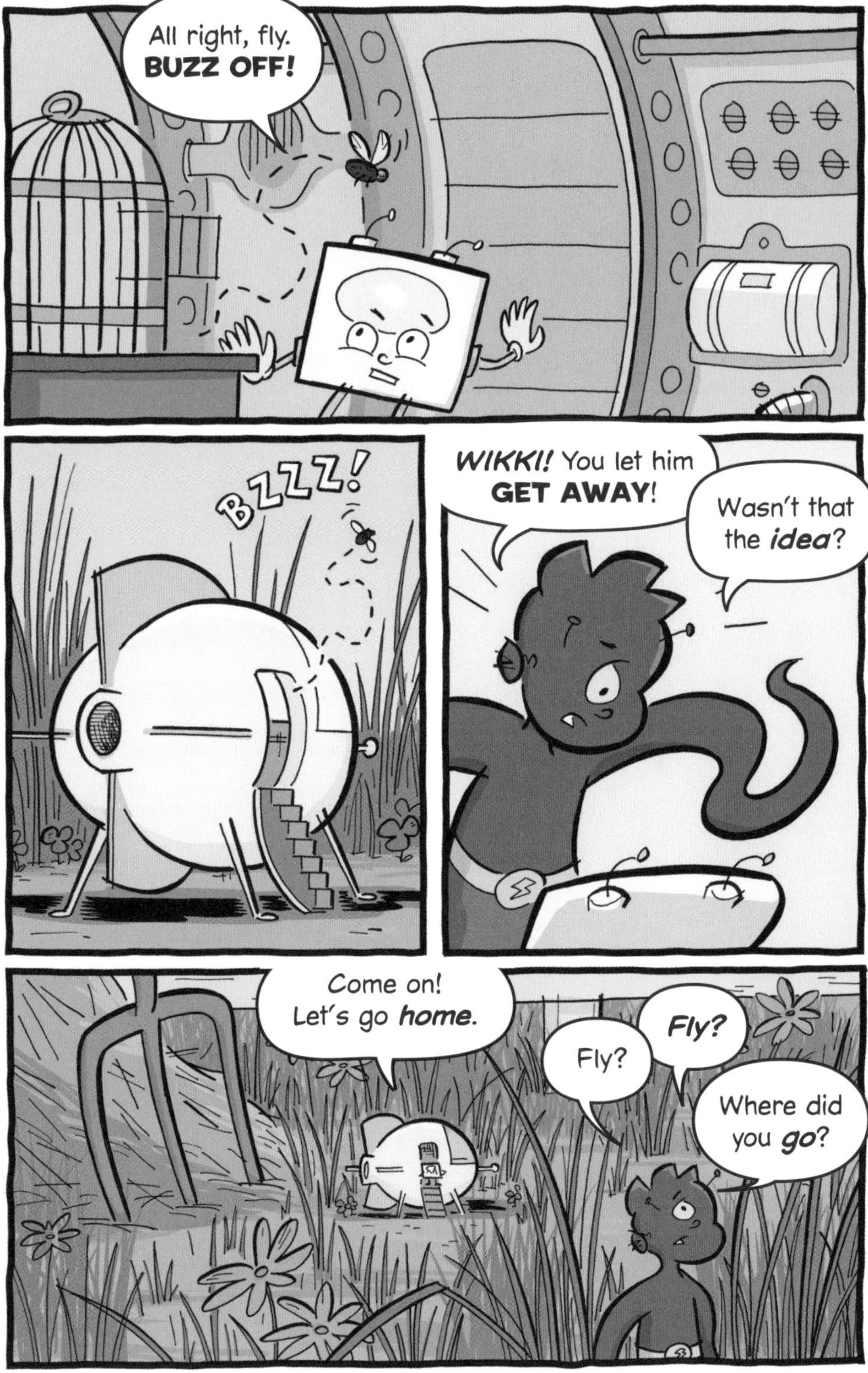
All right, fly. **BUZZ OFF!**
BZZZ!
WIKKI! You let him **GET AWAY**!
Wasn't that the ***idea***?
Come on! Let's go ***home***.
Fly?
Fly?
Where did you ***go***?

Maybe he's around *here*, eating this yummy **GRASS**.

ZIG!

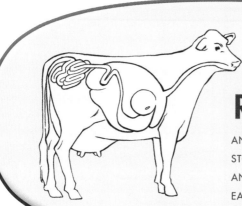

RUMINANTS

ANIMALS WHO HAVE SPECIAL STOMACHS, LIKE COWS, GOATS AND DEER, CAN GET ENERGY FROM EATING GRASS.

So what *do* flies eat?

Who **CARES**!

Mr. Fly? *Here*, boy.

Hey... Zig! Wait for **ME**!

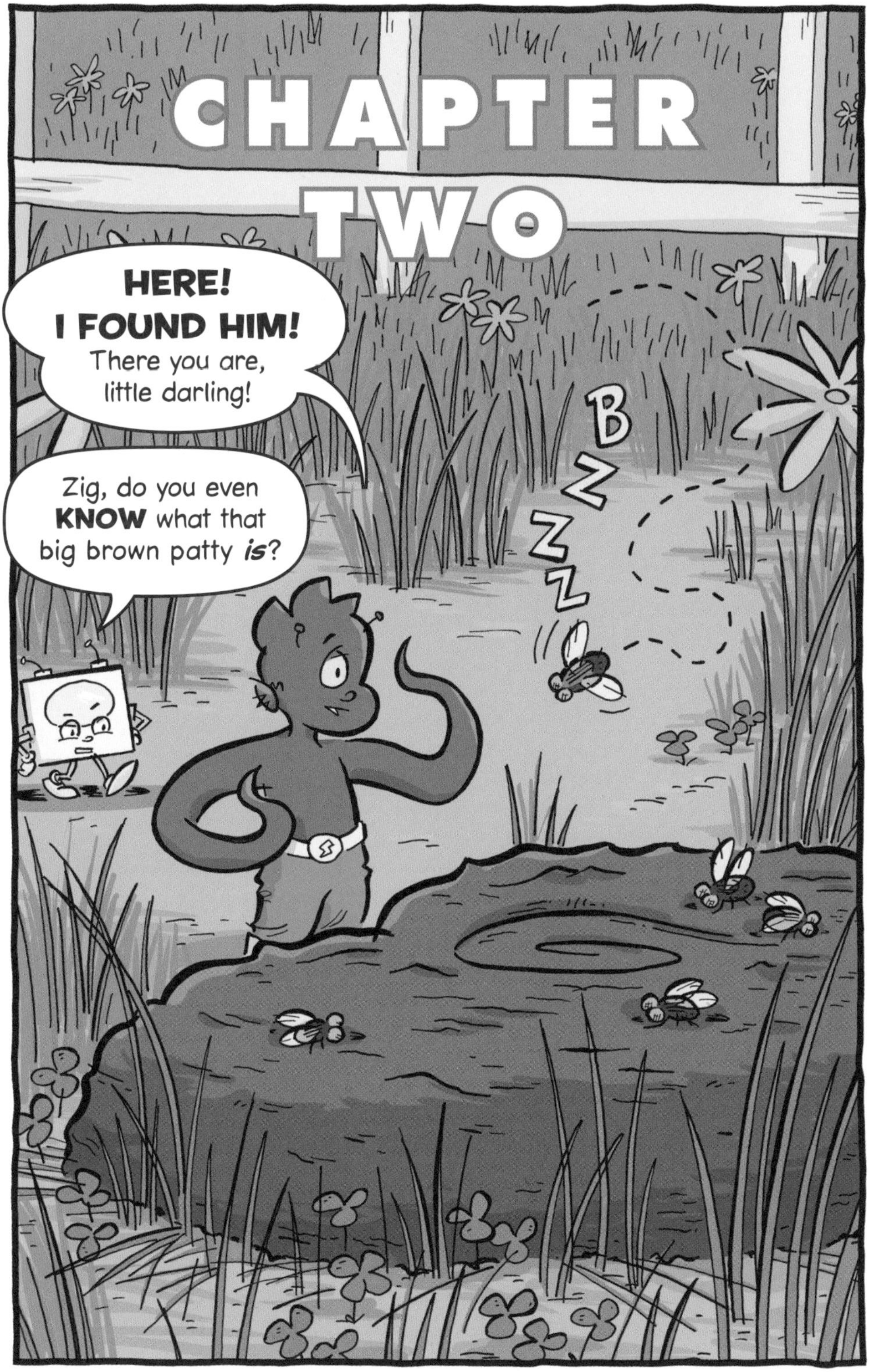
CHAPTER TWO
HERE! I FOUND HIM! There you are, little darling!
Zig, do you even **KNOW** what that big brown patty *is*?
BZZZZ

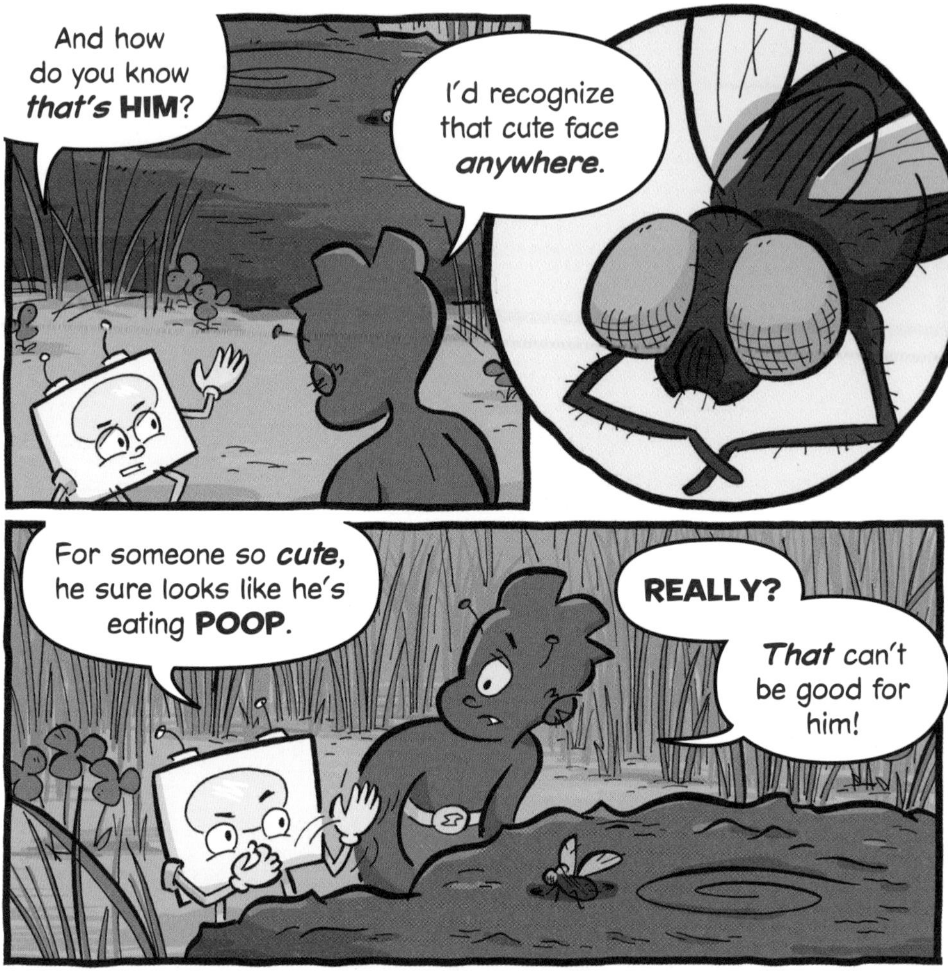
And how do you know *that's* **HIM**?
I'd recognize that cute face *anywhere*.
For someone so *cute*, he sure looks like he's eating **POOP**.
REALLY?
That can't be good for him!

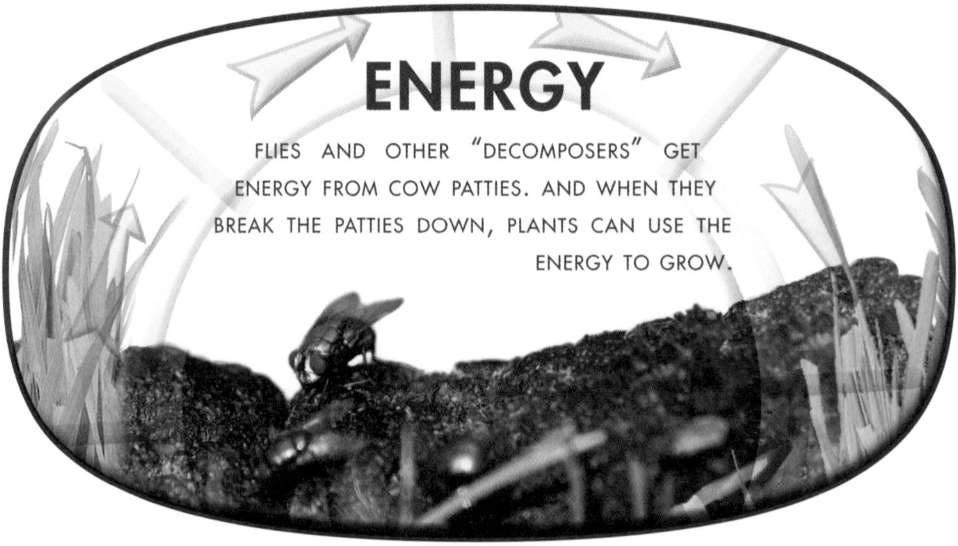
ENERGY
FLIES AND OTHER "DECOMPOSERS" GET ENERGY FROM COW PATTIES. AND WHEN THEY BREAK THE PATTIES DOWN, PLANTS CAN USE THE ENERGY TO GROW.

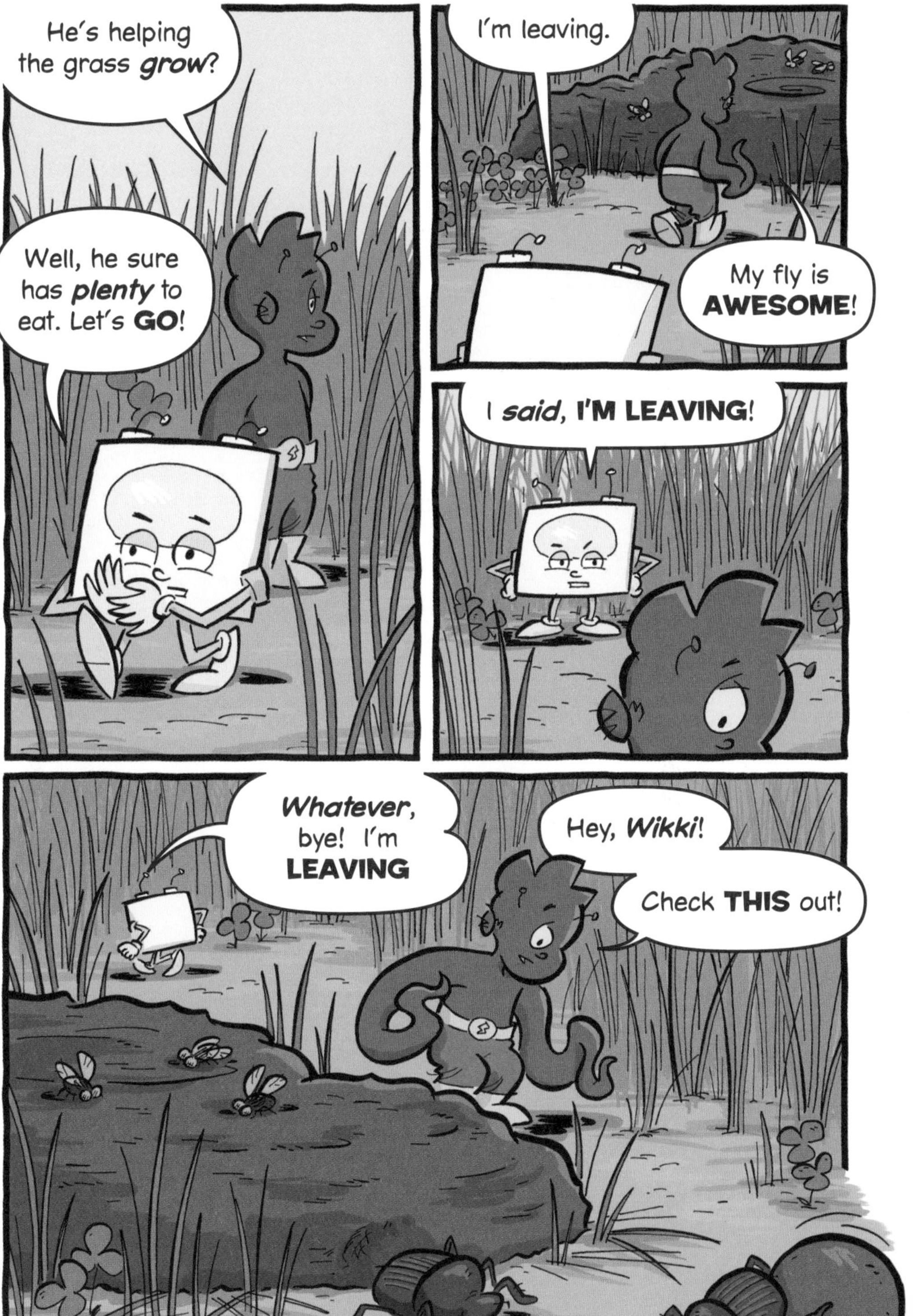
He's helping the grass *grow*?
Well, he sure has *plenty* to eat. Let's **GO**!
I'm leaving.
My fly is **AWESOME**!
I *said*, **I'M LEAVING**!
Whatever, bye! I'm **LEAVING**
Hey, *Wikki*!
Check **THIS** out!

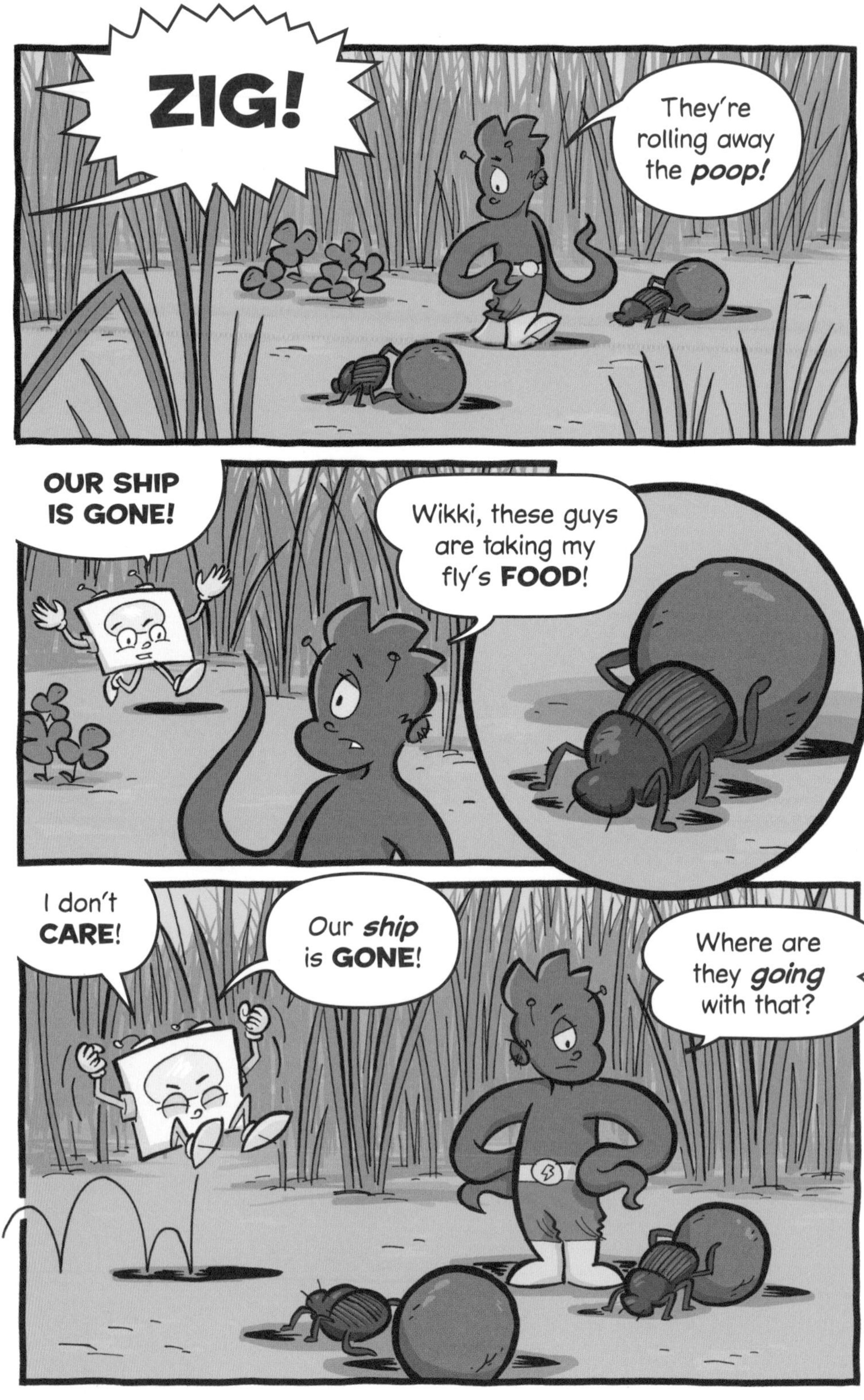
ZIG!
They're rolling away the ***poop!***
OUR SHIP IS GONE!
Wikki, these guys are taking my fly's **FOOD**!
I don't **CARE**!
Our ***ship*** is **GONE**!
Where are they ***going*** with that?

DUNG BEETLES

THERE ARE THREE TYPES OF DUNG BEETLES: *ROLLERS* ROLL BALLS OF DUNG AWAY TO BURY UNDERGROUND, *DWELLERS* LIVE IN THE DUNG, AND *TUNNELERS* BUILD TUNNELS IN THE SOIL.

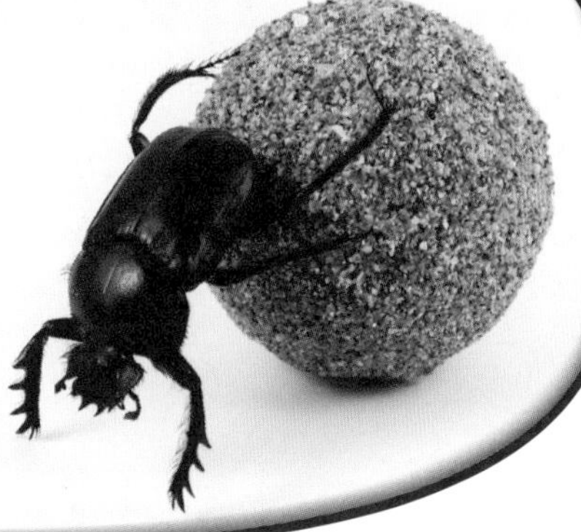

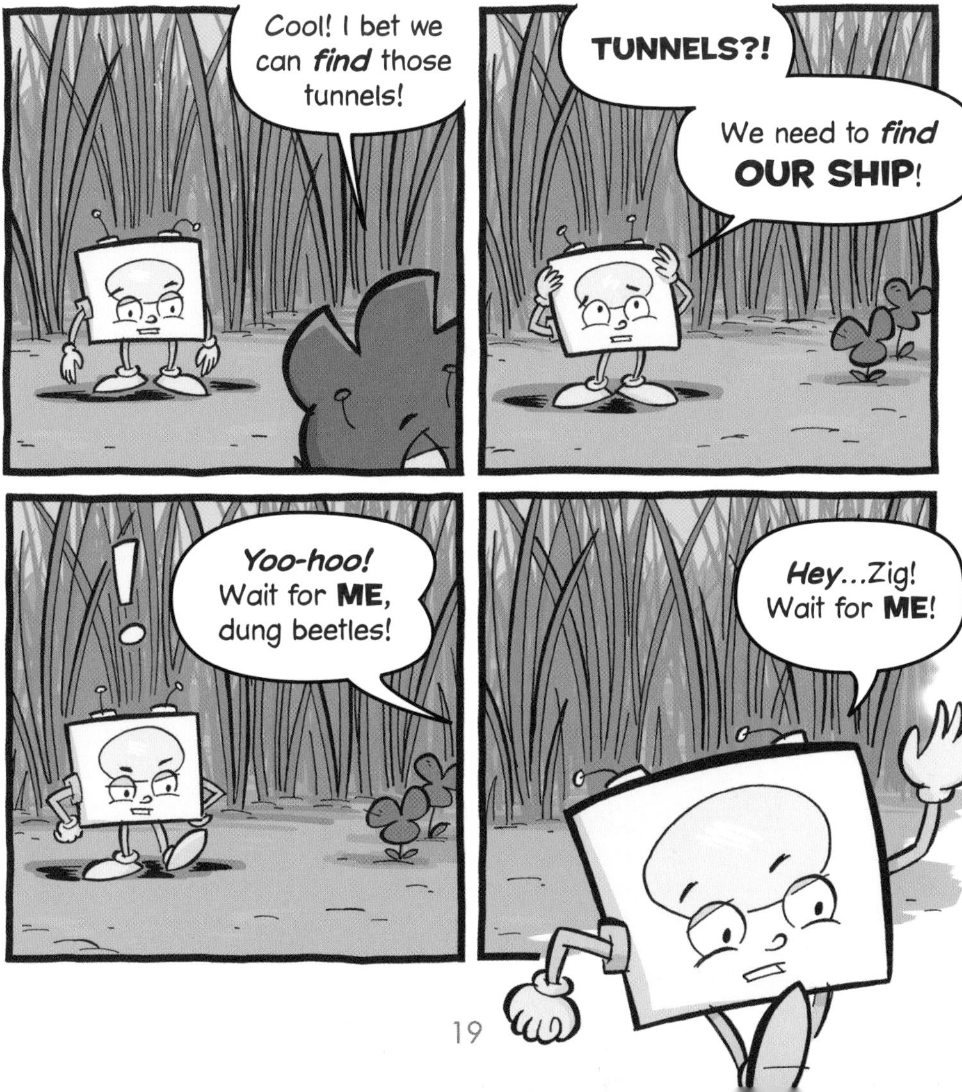

Cool! I bet we can *find* those tunnels!
TUNNELS?!
We need to *find* **OUR SHIP**!
!
Yoo-hoo! Wait for **ME**, dung beetles!
Hey...Zig! Wait for **ME**!

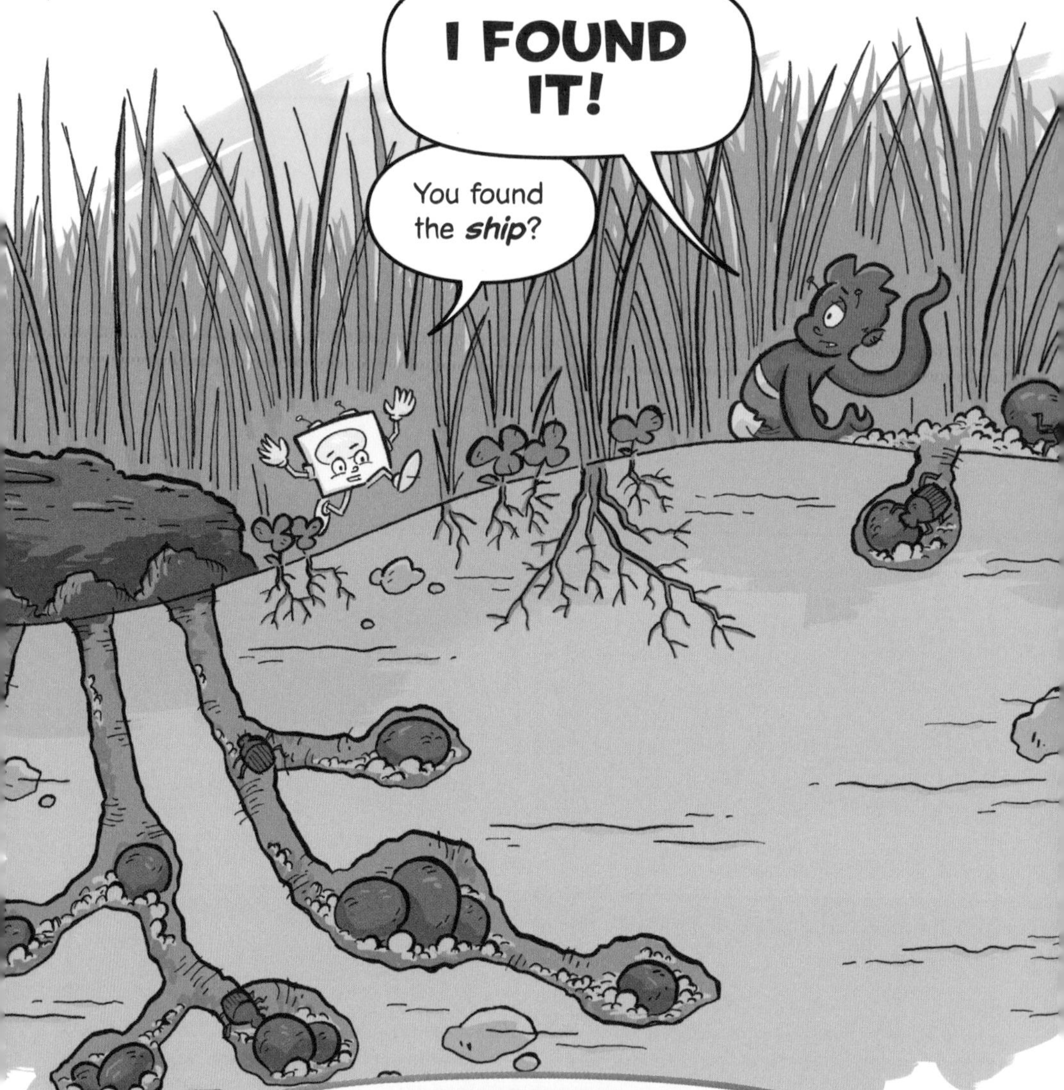
I FOUND IT!
You found the ***ship***?

DECOMPOSERS

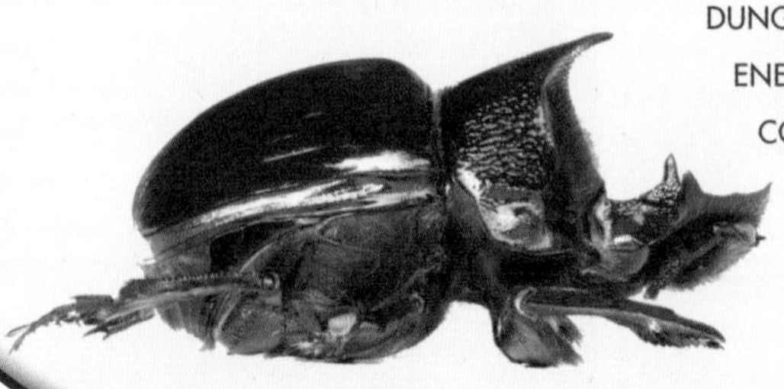

DUNG BEETLES MAKE USE OF THE ENERGY IN THE GRASS LEFT IN A COW'S DUNG. THEY ALSO LAY THEIR EGGS INSIDE IT.

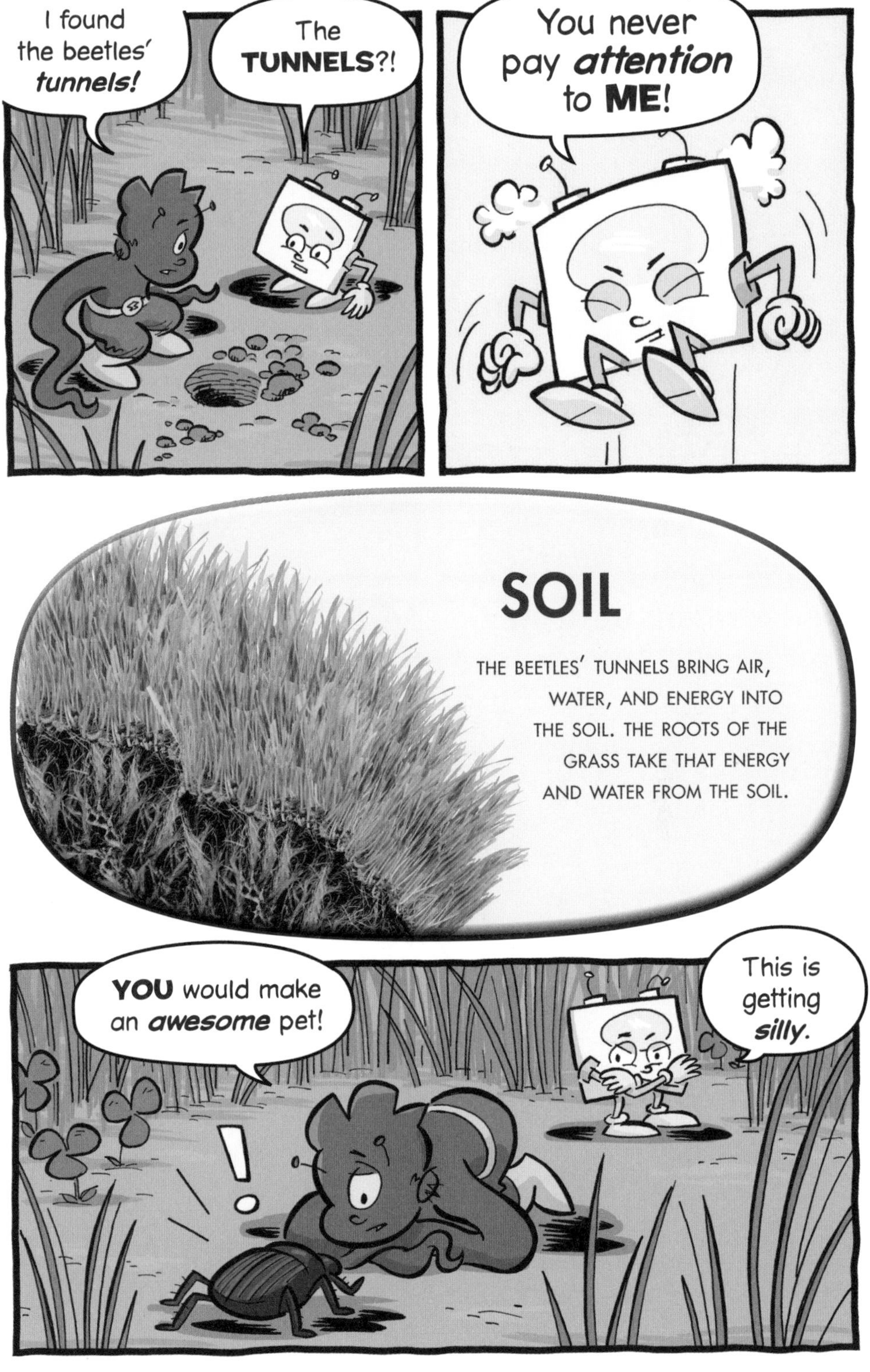
I found the beetles' *tunnels!*
The **TUNNELS**?!
You never pay ***attention*** to **ME**!
SOIL
THE BEETLES' TUNNELS BRING AIR, WATER, AND ENERGY INTO THE SOIL. THE ROOTS OF THE GRASS TAKE THAT ENERGY AND WATER FROM THE SOIL.
YOU would make an ***awesome*** pet!
!
This is getting ***silly***.

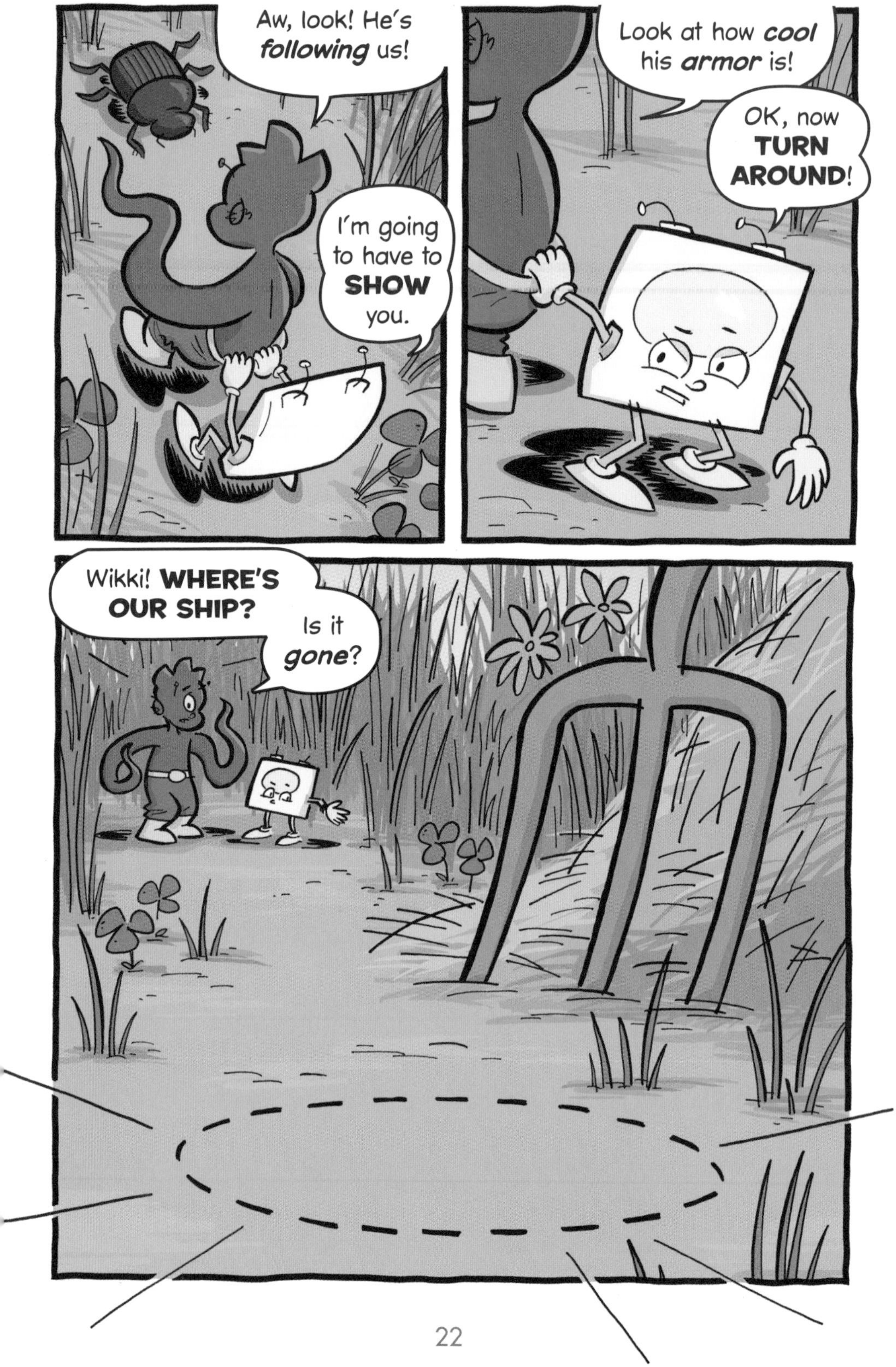
Aw, look! He's *following* us!
I'm going to have to **SHOW** you.
Look at how *cool* his *armor* is!
OK, now **TURN AROUND**!
Wikki! **WHERE'S OUR SHIP?**
Is it *gone*?

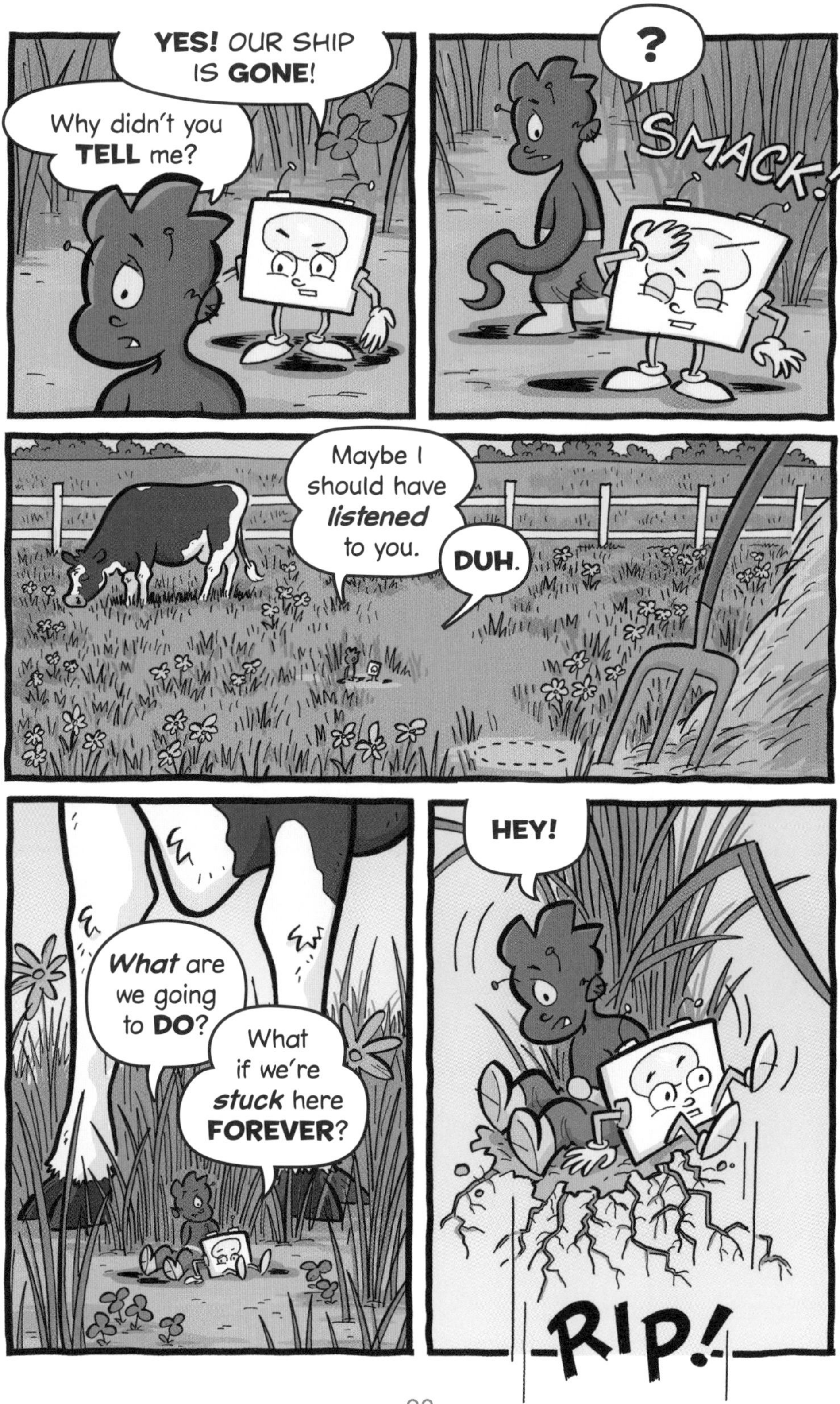
YES! OUR SHIP IS GONE!
Why didn't you TELL me?
?
SMACK!
Maybe I should have listened to you.
DUH.
What are we going to DO?
What if we're stuck here FOREVER?
HEY!
RIP!

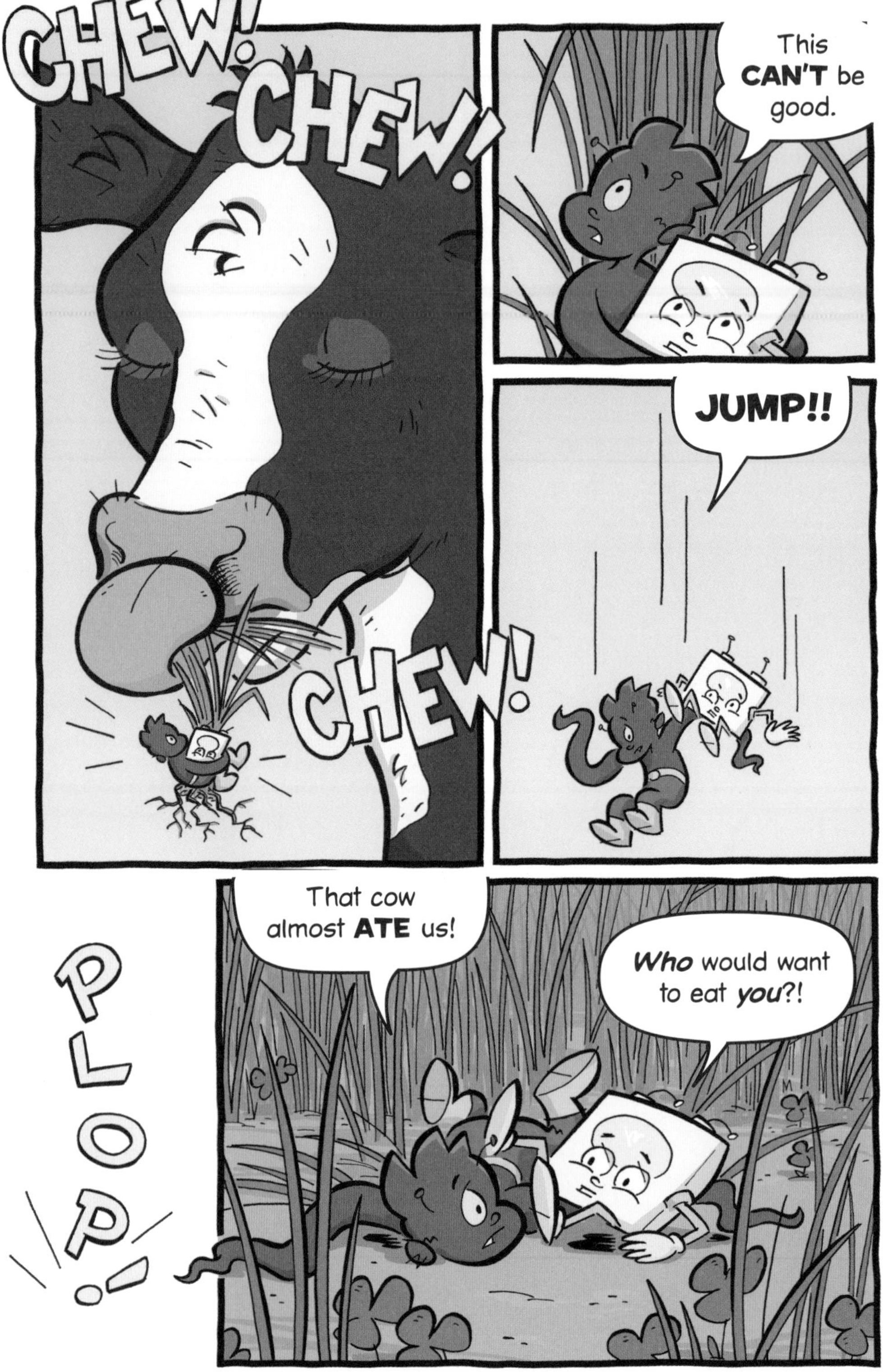
CHEW! CHEW!
CHEW!
This CAN'T be good.
JUMP!!
PLOP!
That cow almost ATE us!
Who would want to eat you?!

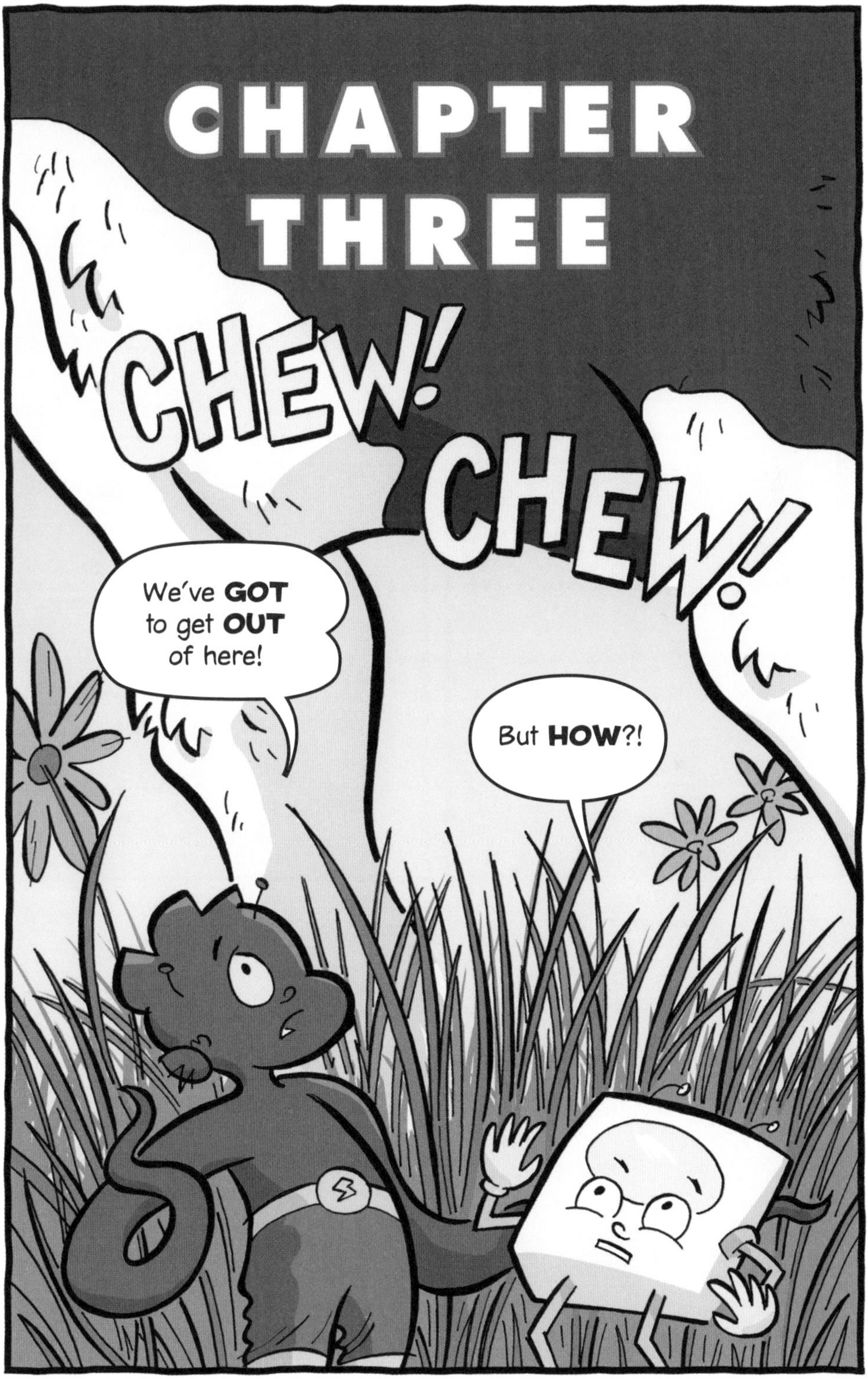
CHAPTER THREE
CHEW!
CHEW!
We've GOT to get OUT of here!
But HOW?!

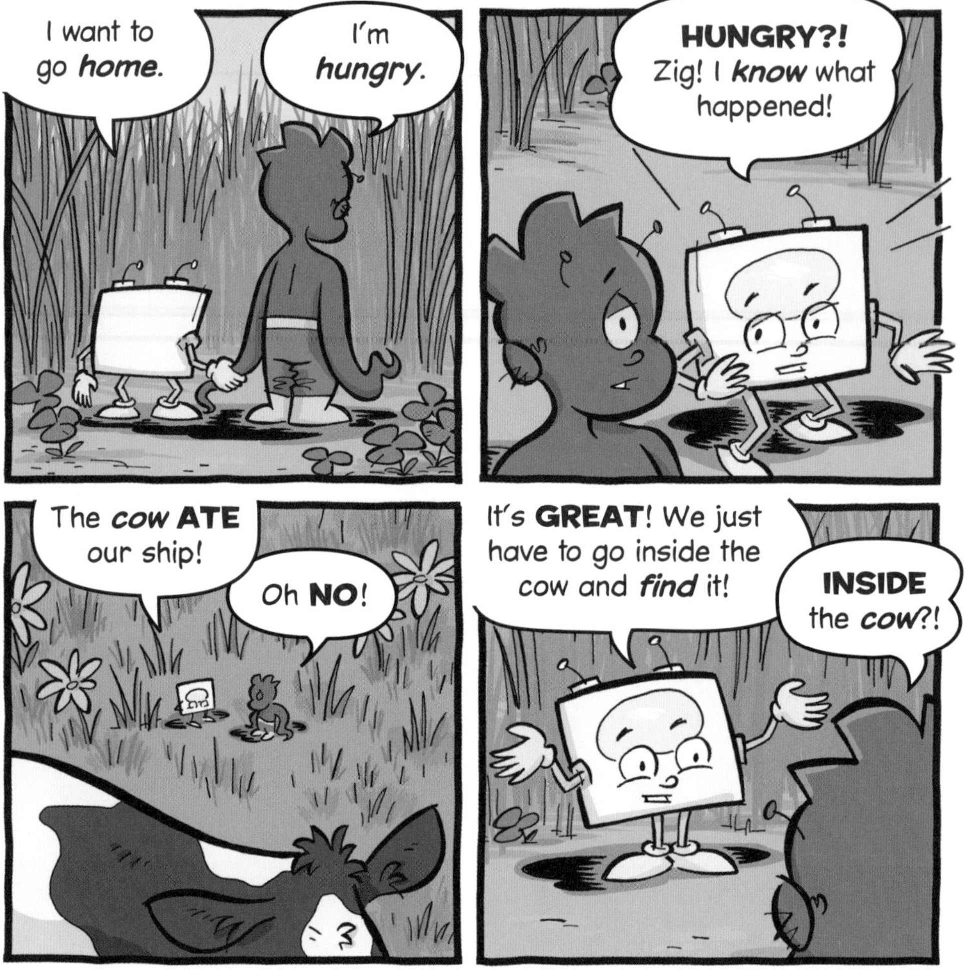
I want to go *home*.
I'm *hungry*.
HUNGRY?! Zig! I *know* what happened!
The *cow* **ATE** our ship!
Oh **NO**!
It's **GREAT**! We just have to go inside the cow and *find* it!
INSIDE the *cow*?!

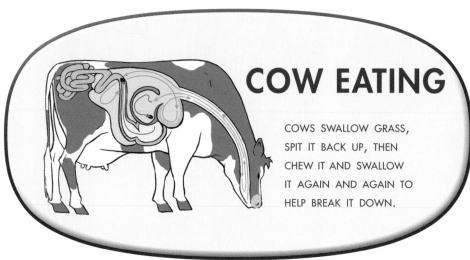

COW EATING

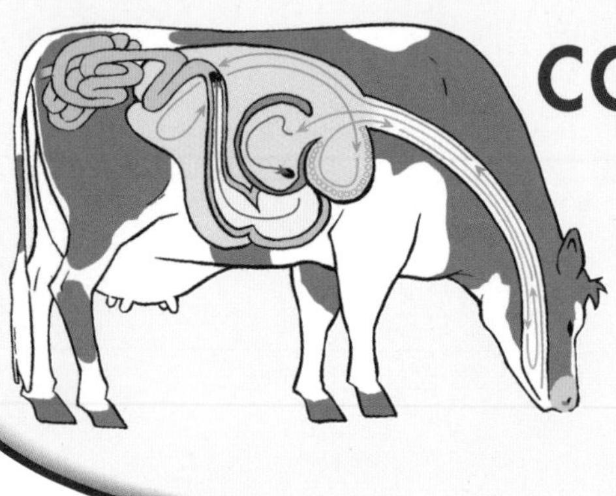

COWS SWALLOW GRASS, SPIT IT BACK UP, THEN CHEW IT AND SWALLOW IT AGAIN AND AGAIN TO HELP BREAK IT DOWN.

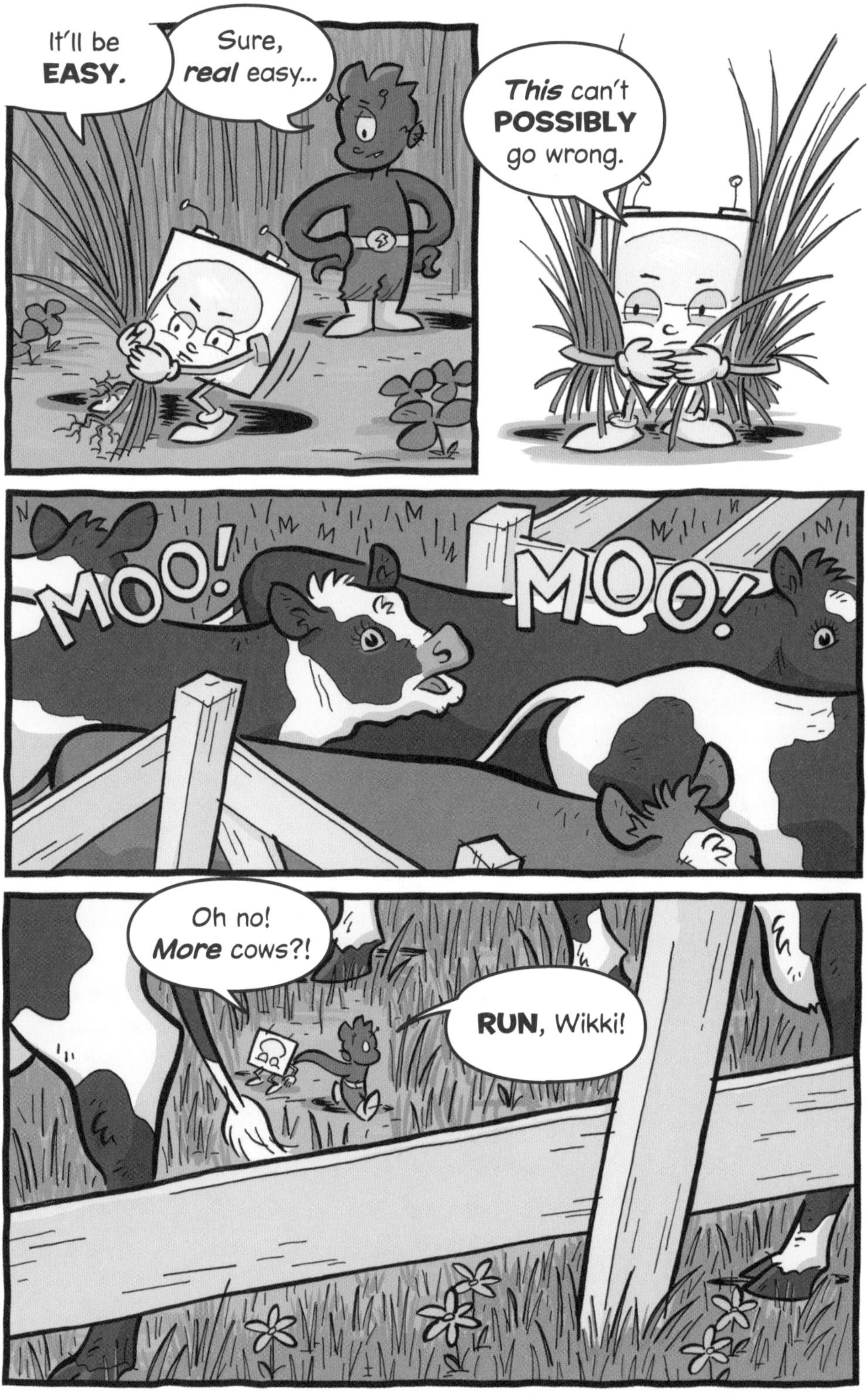
It'll be **EASY.**
Sure, ***real*** easy...
This can't **POSSIBLY** go wrong.
MOO!
MOO!
Oh no! ***More*** cows?!
RUN, Wikki!

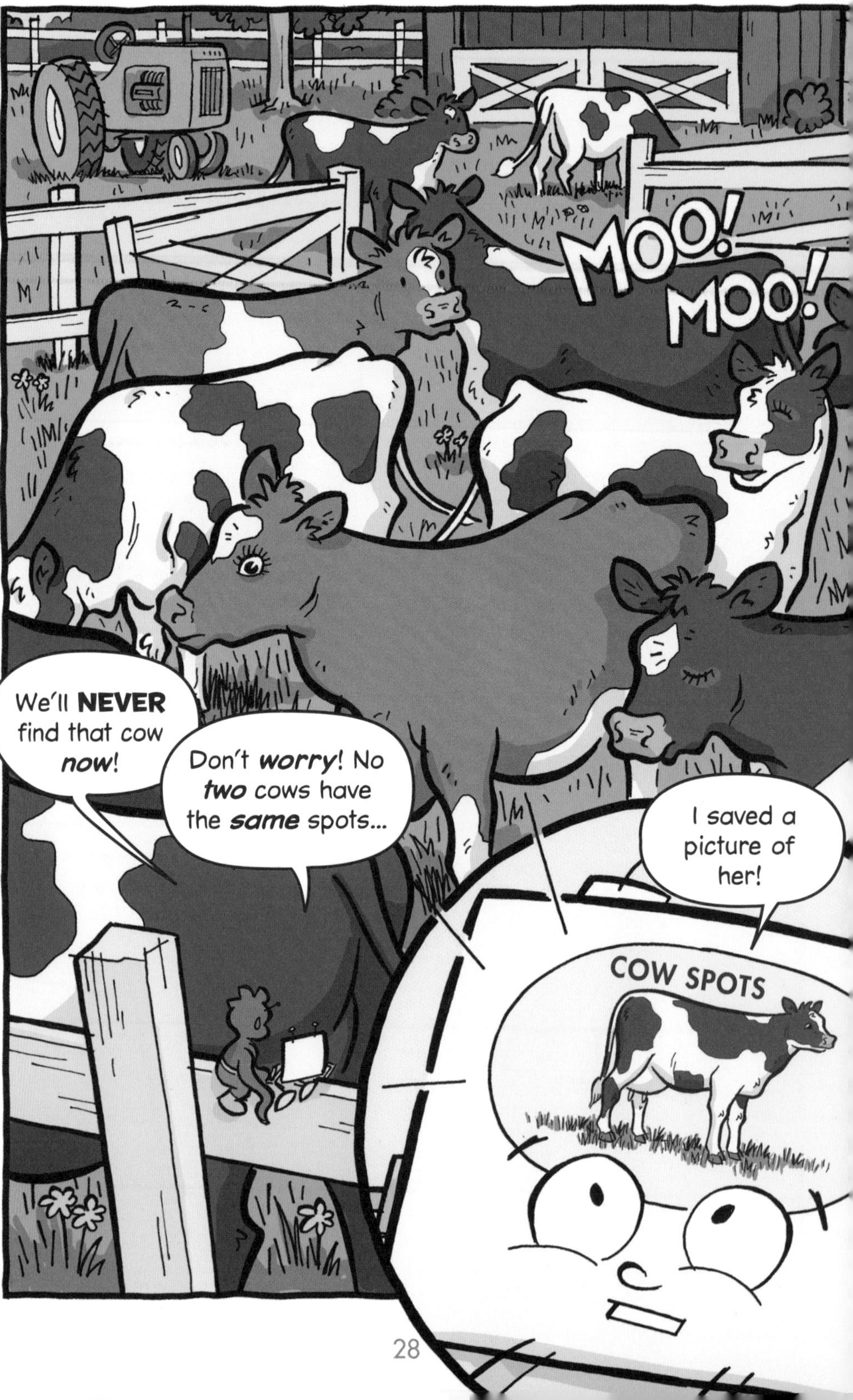
MOO!
MOO!
We'll **NEVER** find that cow *now*!
Don't *worry*! No *two* cows have the *same* spots...
I saved a picture of her!
COW SPOTS

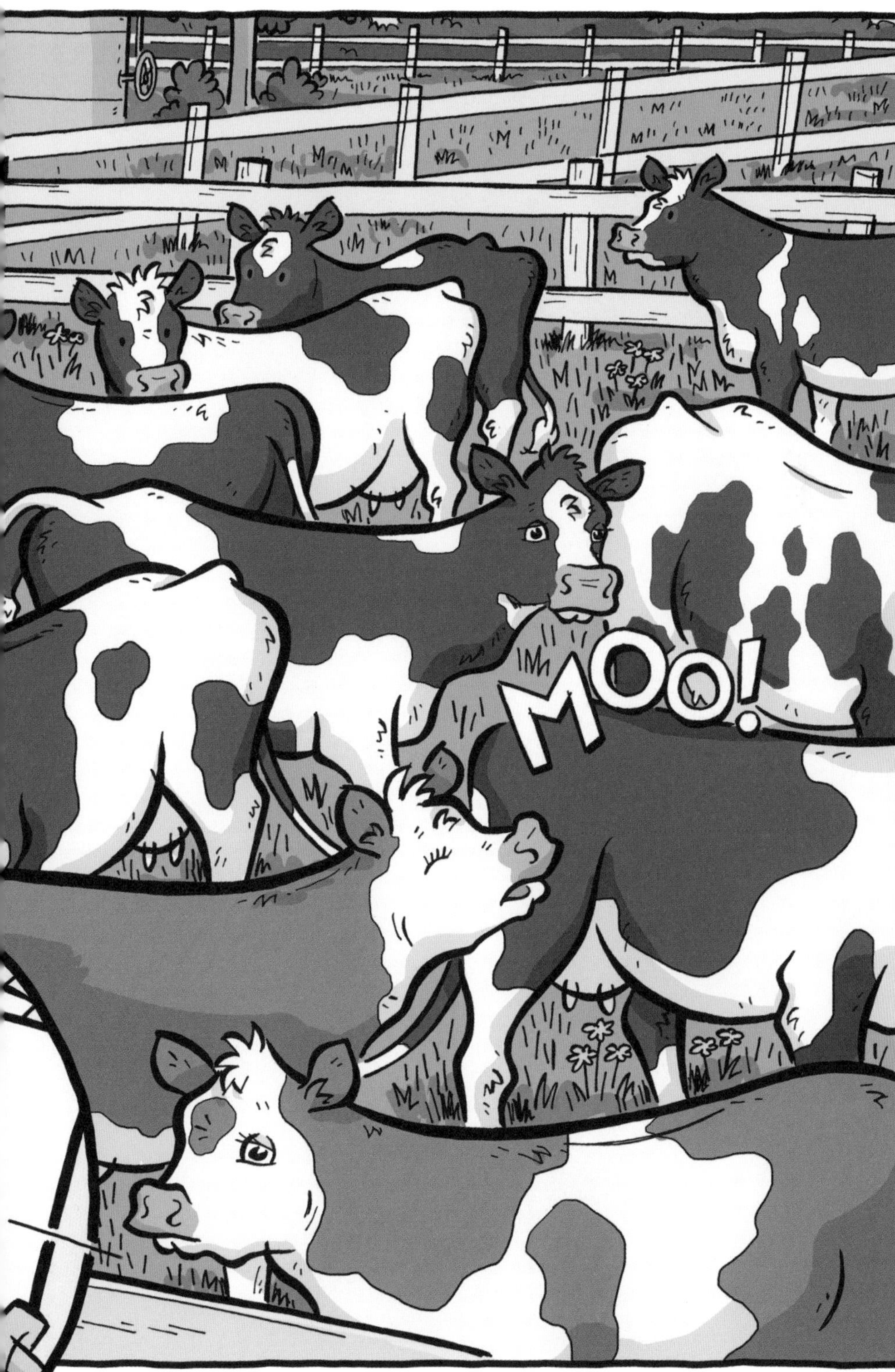
MOO!

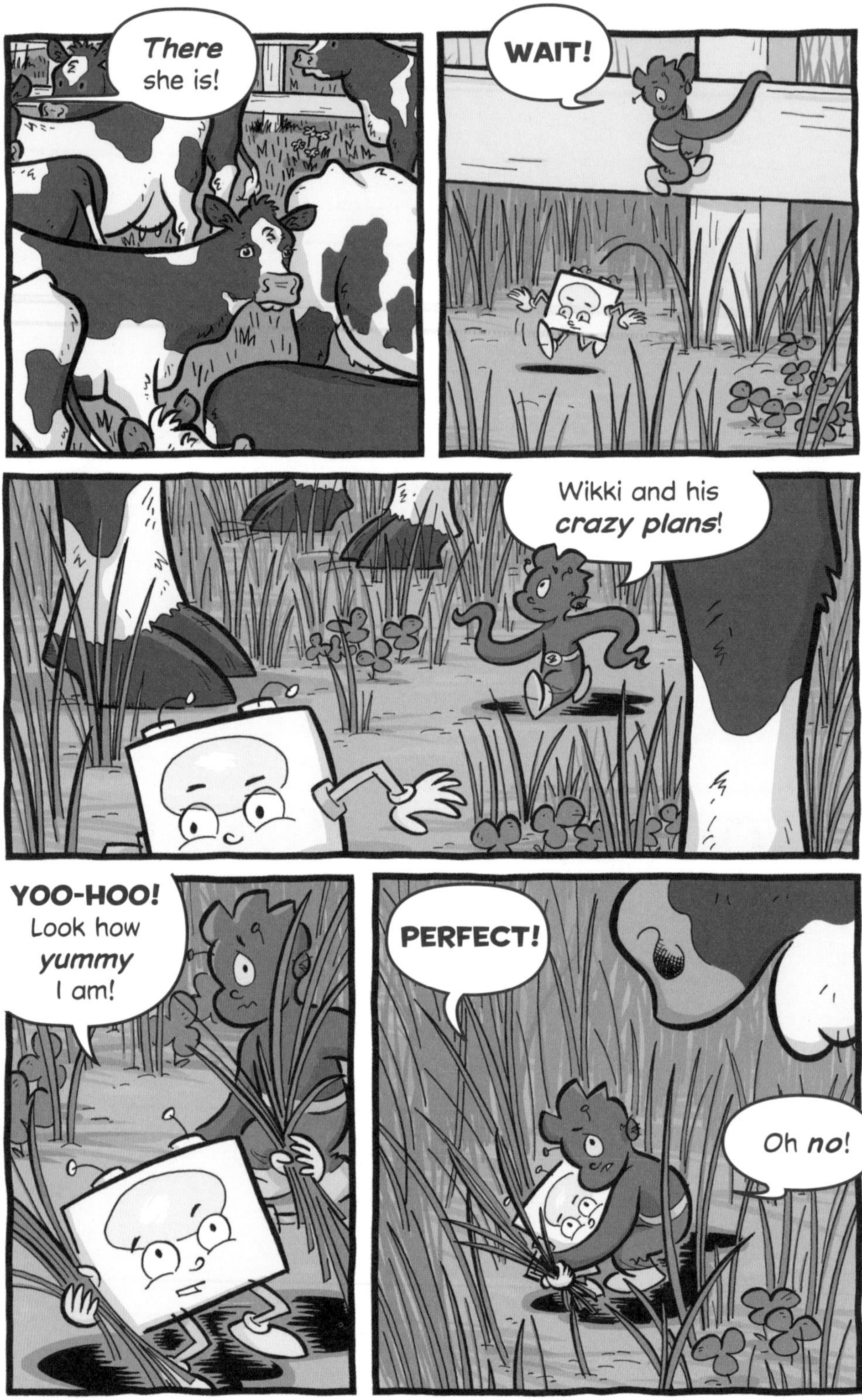
There she is!
WAIT!
Wikki and his *crazy plans*!
YOO-HOO! Look how *yummy* I am!
PERFECT!
Oh *no*!

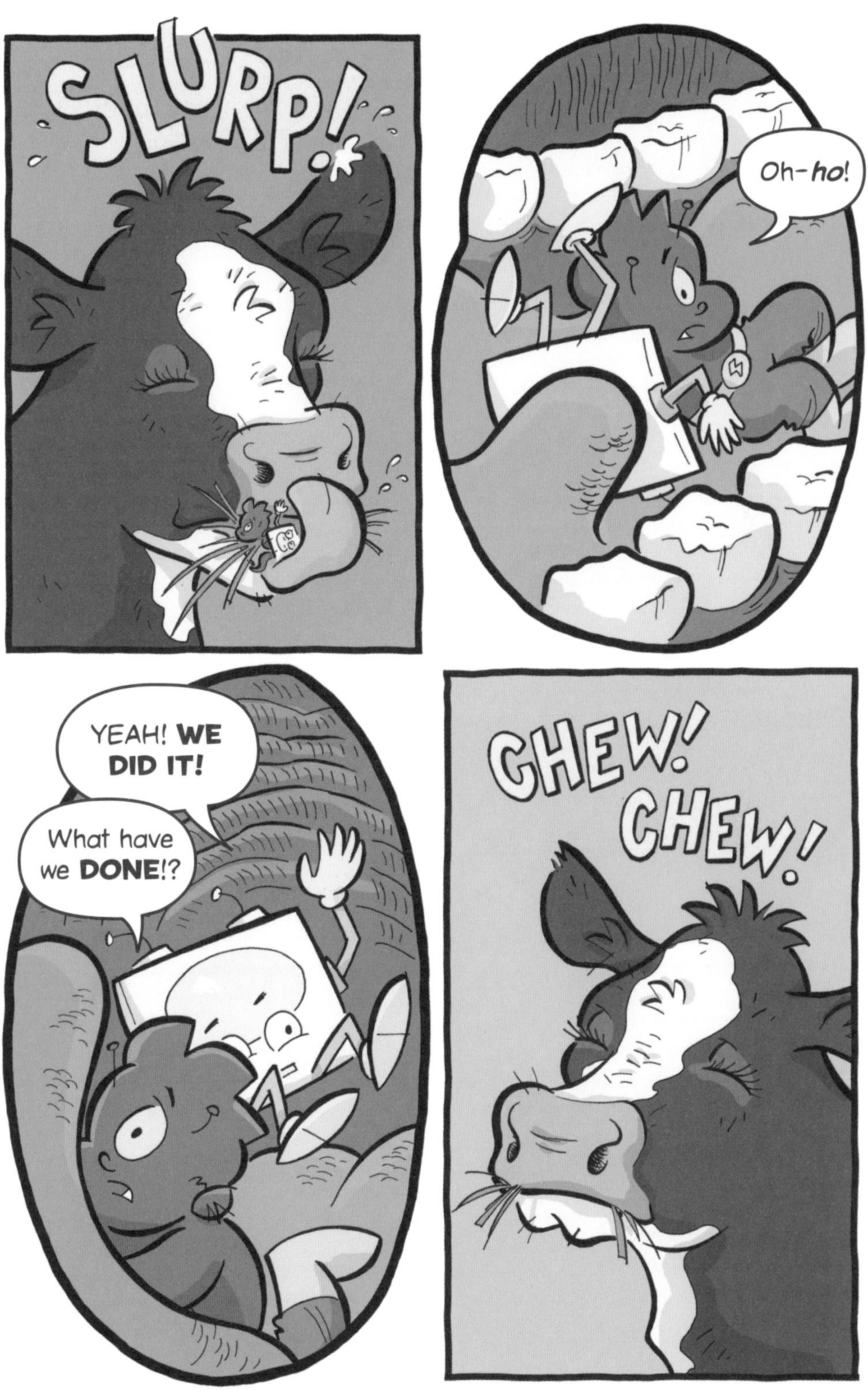
SLURP!
Oh-ho!
YEAH! WE DID IT!
What have we DONE!?
CHEW! CHEW!

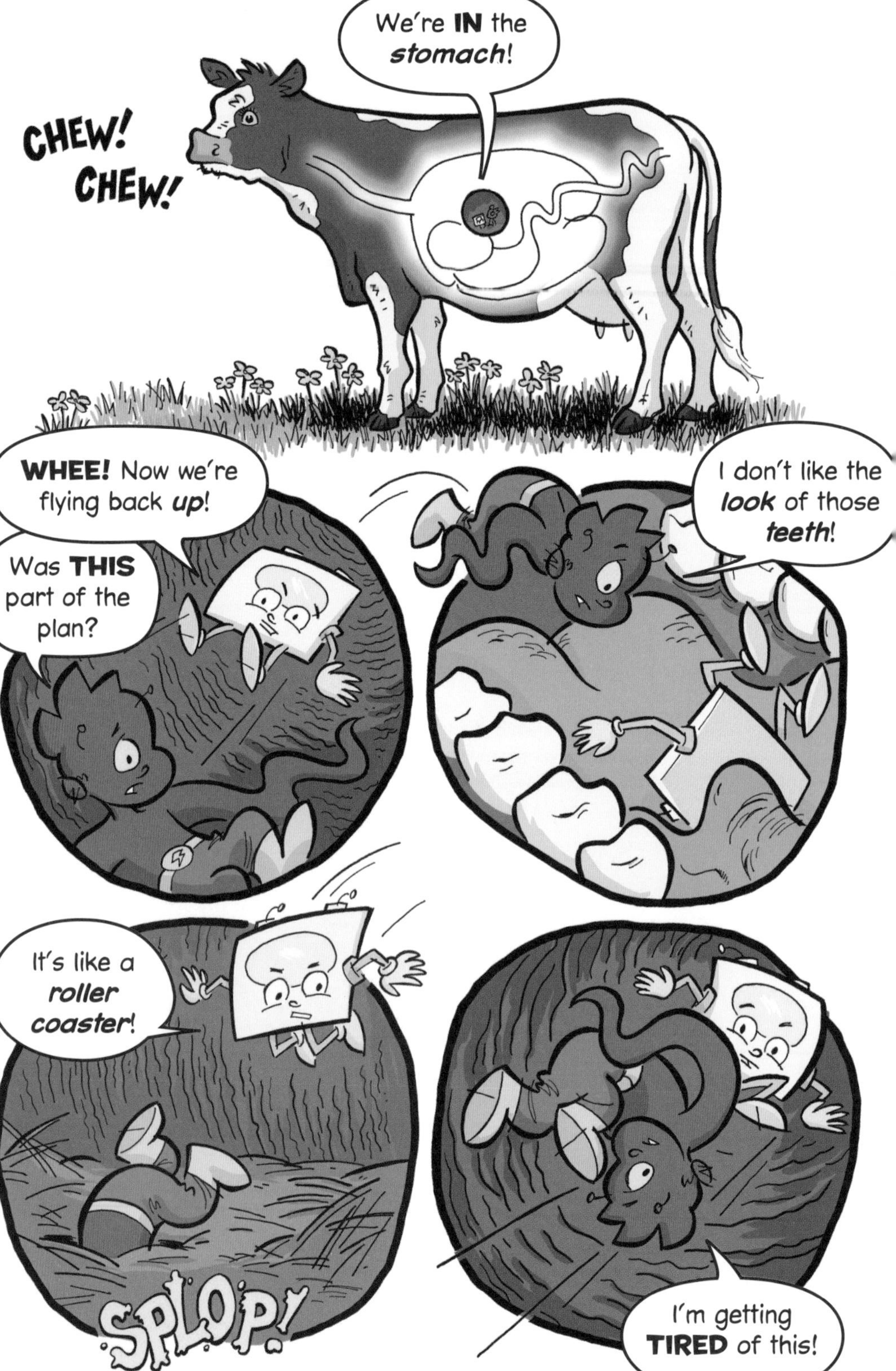
We're **IN** the ***stomach***!
CHEW! CHEW!
WHEE! Now we're flying back ***up***!
Was **THIS** part of the plan?
I don't like the ***look*** of those ***teeth***!
It's like a ***roller coaster***!
SPLOP!
I'm getting **TIRED** of this!

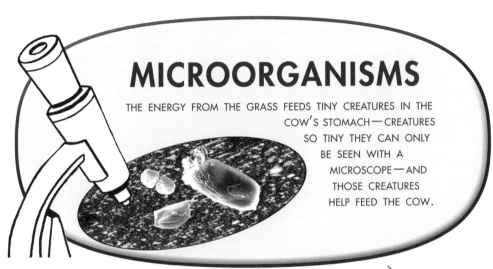

MICROORGANISMS

THE ENERGY FROM THE GRASS FEEDS TINY CREATURES IN THE COW'S STOMACH — CREATURES SO TINY THEY CAN ONLY BE SEEN WITH A MICROSCOPE — AND THOSE CREATURES HELP FEED THE COW.

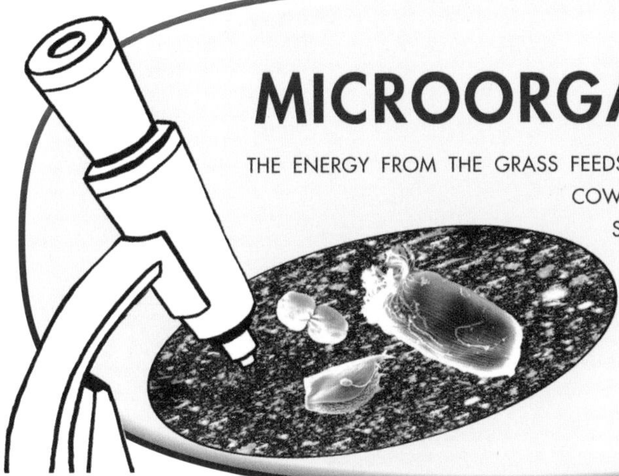

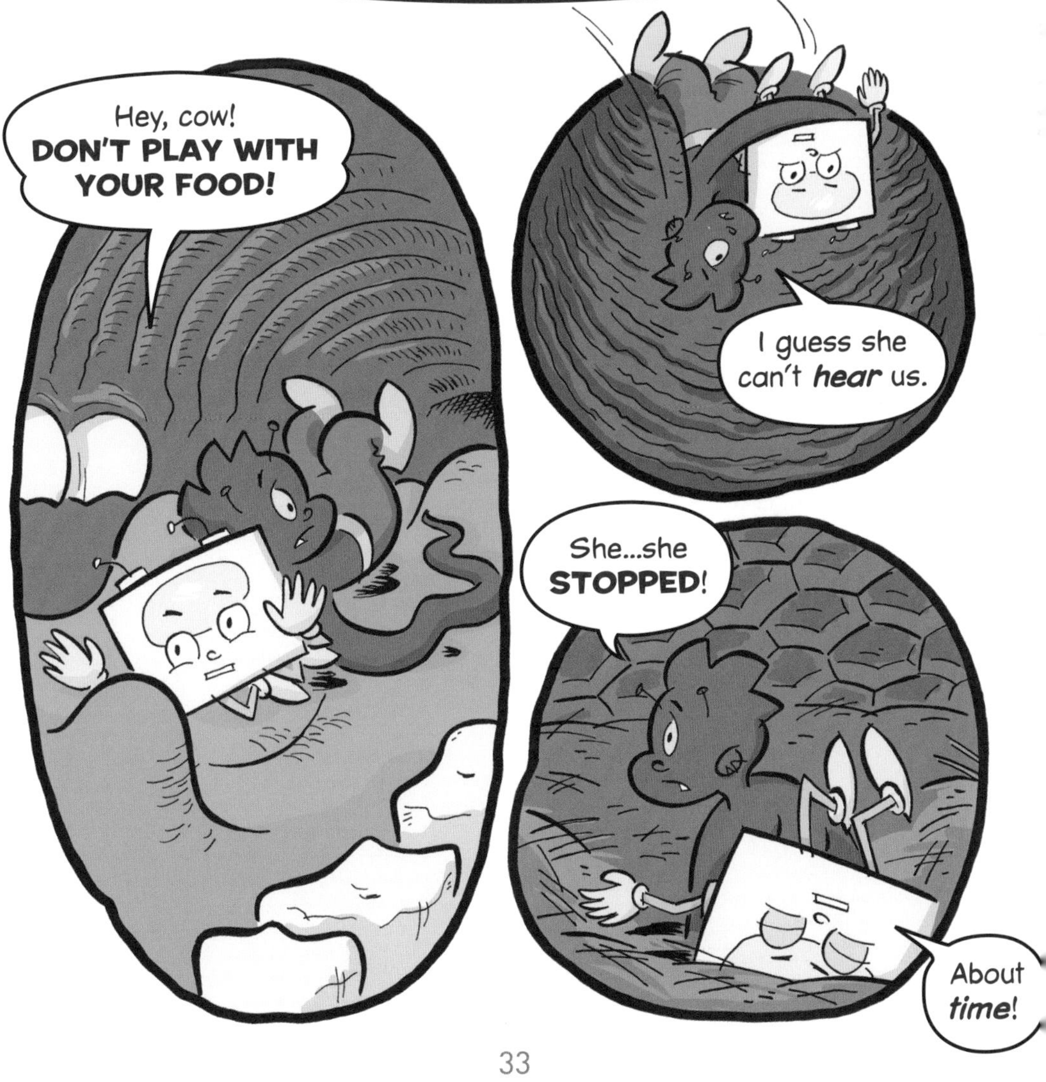
Hey, cow!
DON'T PLAY WITH YOUR FOOD!
I guess she can't ***hear*** us.
She...she **STOPPED**!
About ***time***!

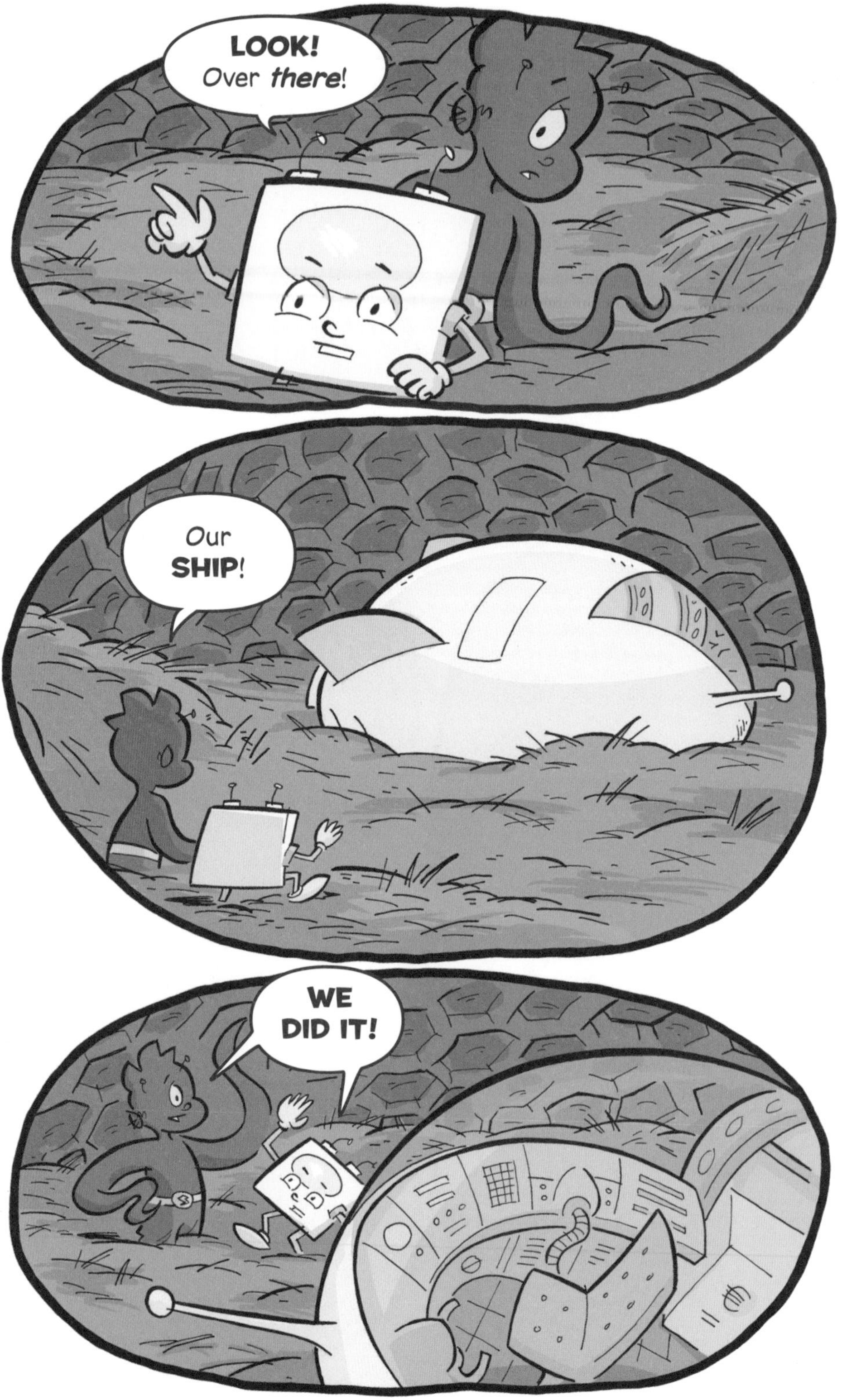
LOOK!
Over *there*!
Our **SHIP**!
WE DID IT!

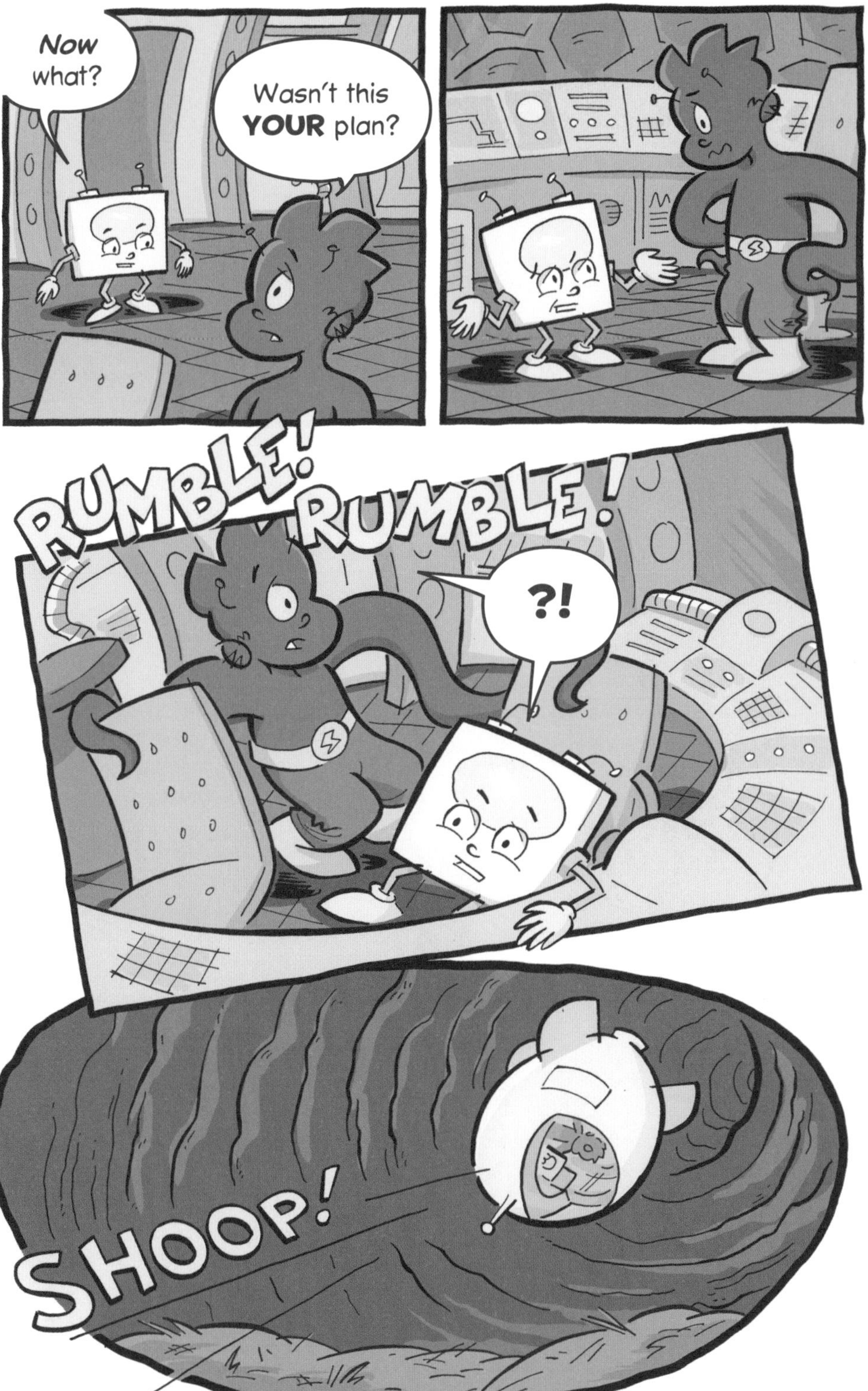
Now what?
Wasn't this YOUR plan?
RUMBLE! RUMBLE!
?!
SHOOP!

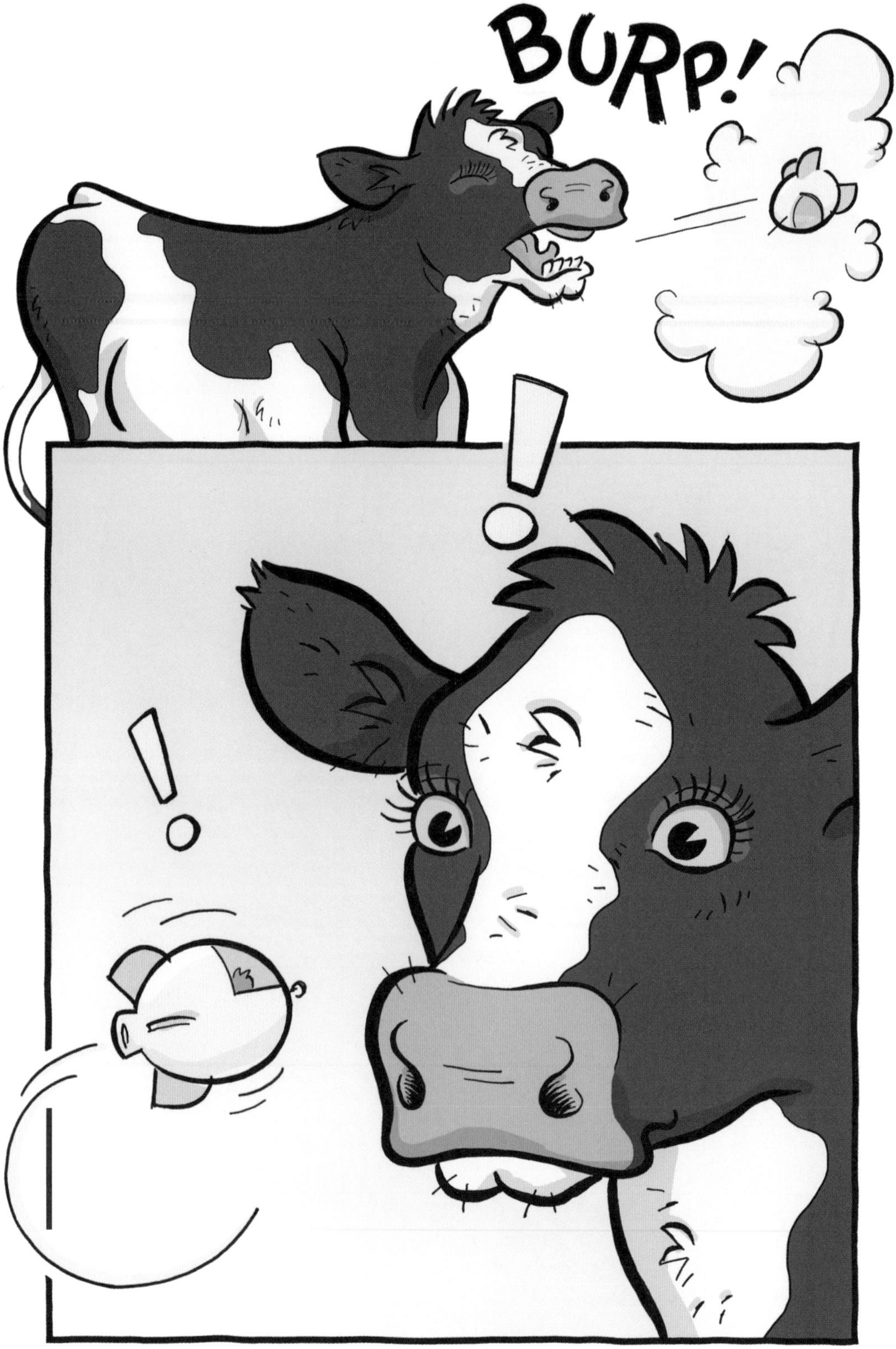
BURP!
!
!

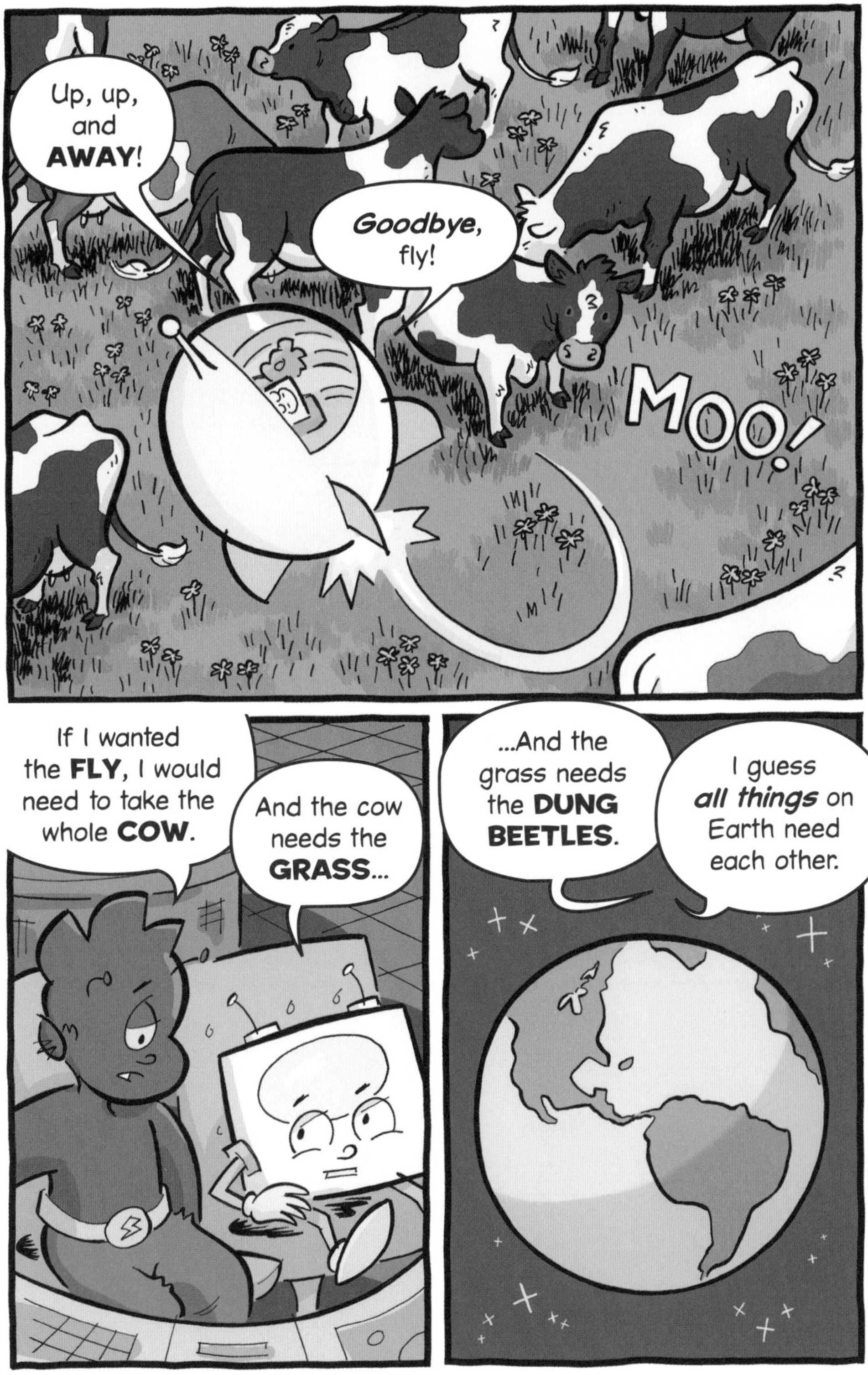
Up, up, and **AWAY**!
Goodbye, fly!
MOO!
If I wanted the **FLY**, I would need to take the whole **COW**.
And the cow needs the **GRASS**...
...And the grass needs the **DUNG BEETLES**.
I guess ***all things*** on Earth need each other.

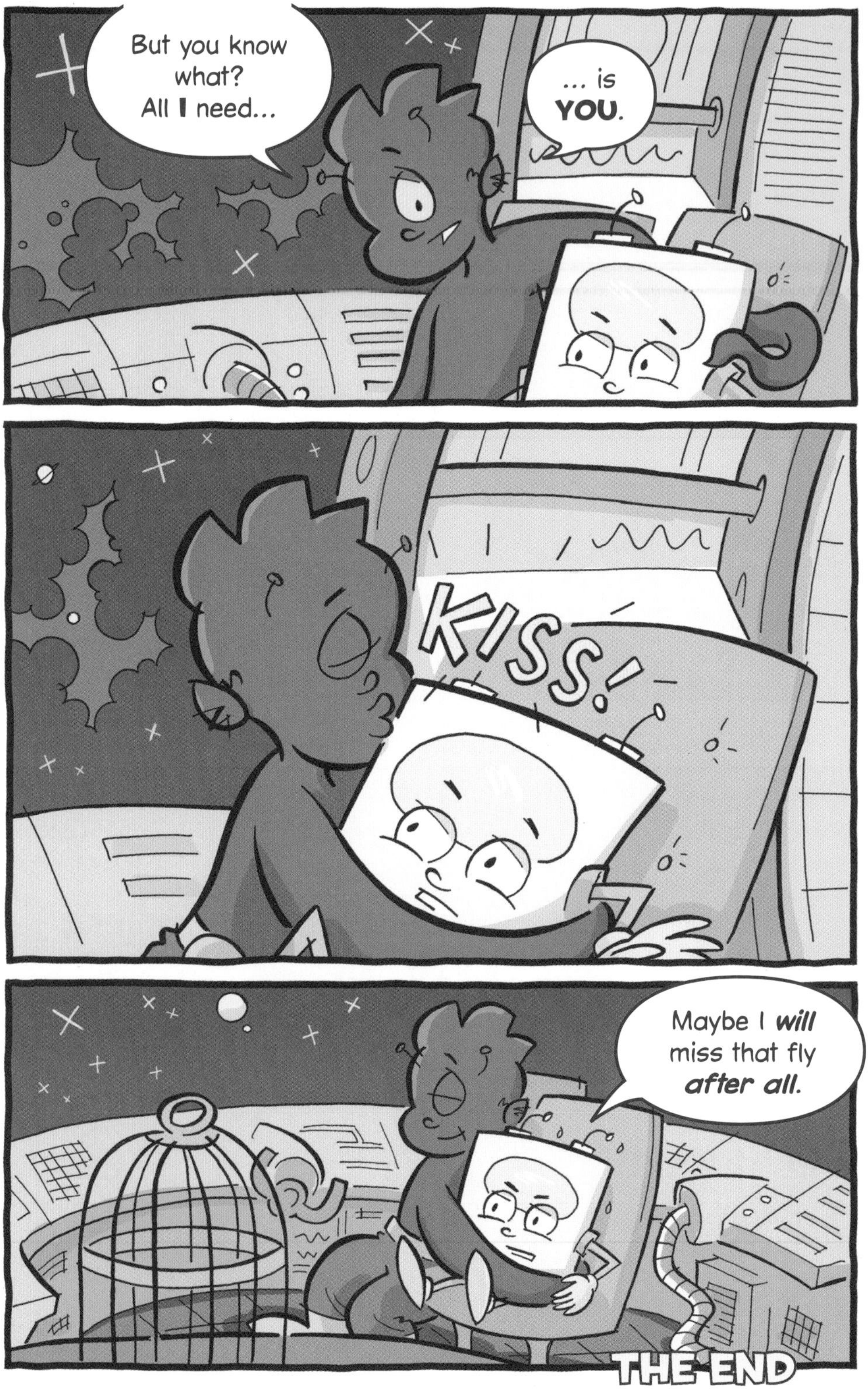
But you know what? All **I** need...
... is **YOU**.
KISS!
Maybe I ***will*** miss that fly ***after all.***
THE END

ABOUT THE AUTHORS

NADJA SPIEGELMAN, who writes Zig and Wikki's adventures, likes cooking, writing, and decorating her apartment with furniture found on the street. She grew up in New York City, but loves going on vacation to the countryside. Once, when she was very young, a cow mistook her bright yellow dress for a flower and tried to eat her. She's still a little afraid of cows, but she'd like to learn how to milk one.

TRADE LOEFFLER, who draws Zig and Wikki, lives in Brooklyn, New York, with his wife, son, and their dog, Boo. Trade grew up in Livermore, California, the home of "the World's Fastest Rodeo," an event complete with bull riding and wild cow milking. Although he grew up in a "cow town," Trade has never considered himself a cowboy—even though he does own two pairs of cowboy boots.

WIKKI'S FUN FACTS

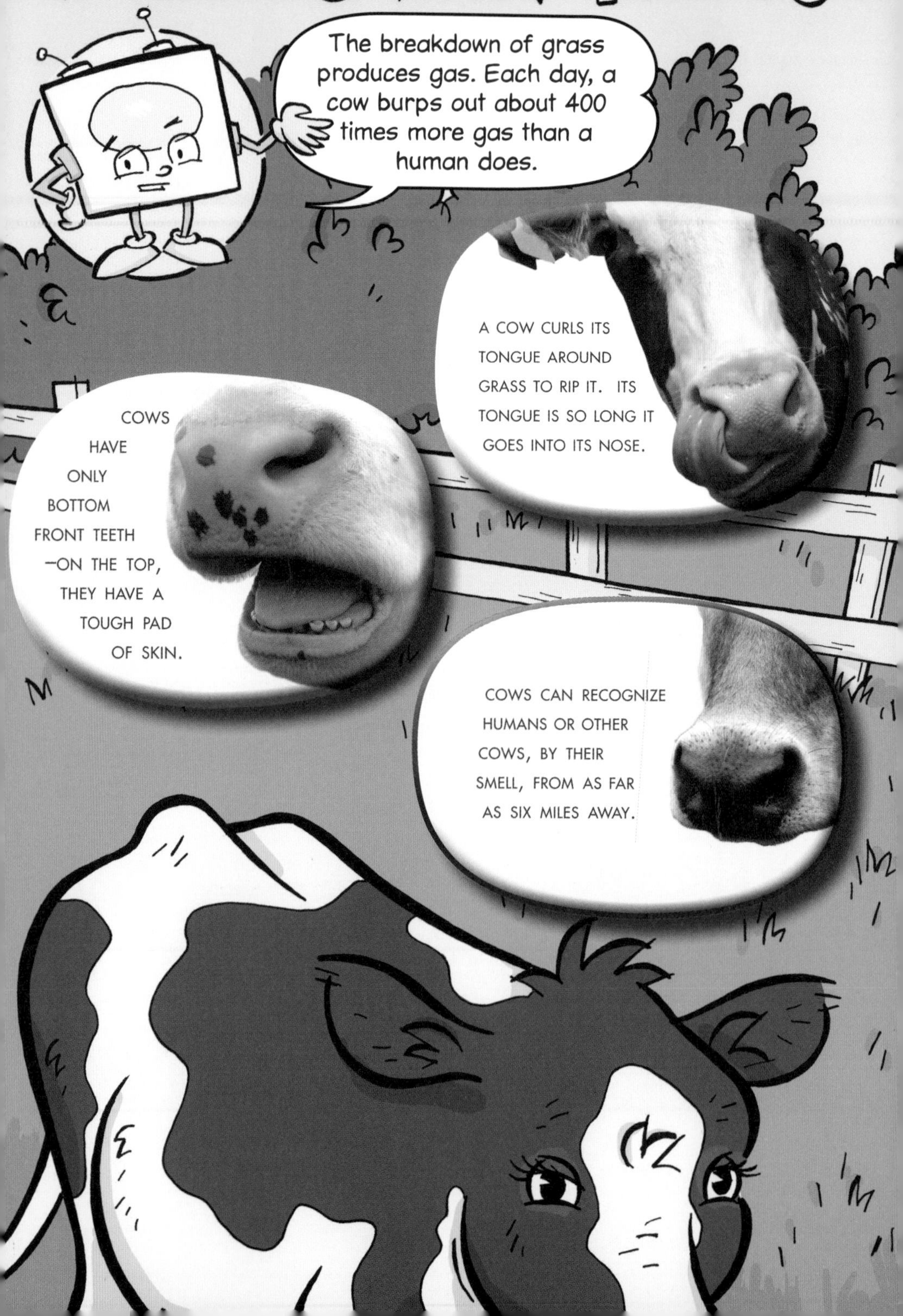
The breakdown of grass produces gas. Each day, a cow burps out about 400 times more gas than a human does.
A COW CURLS ITS TONGUE AROUND GRASS TO RIP IT. ITS TONGUE IS SO LONG IT GOES INTO ITS NOSE.
COWS HAVE ONLY BOTTOM FRONT TEETH —ON THE TOP, THEY HAVE A TOUGH PAD OF SKIN.
COWS CAN RECOGNIZE HUMANS OR OTHER COWS, BY THEIR SMELL, FROM AS FAR AS SIX MILES AWAY.

What works?
Keep your fingertip below the character that is speaking.

3 GUIDE YOUNG READERS

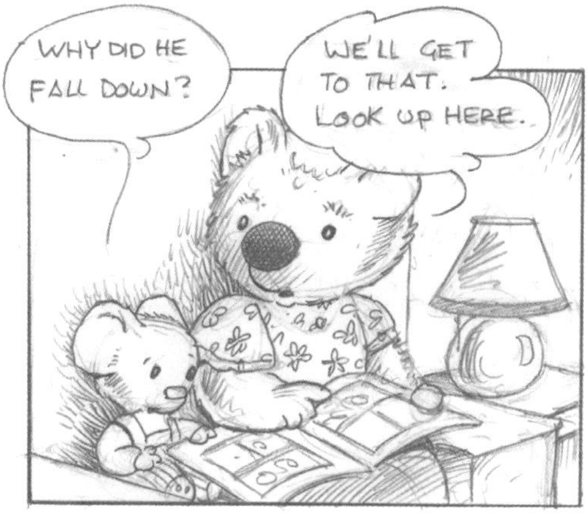
WHY DID HE FALL DOWN?
WE'LL GET TO THAT. LOOK UP HERE.

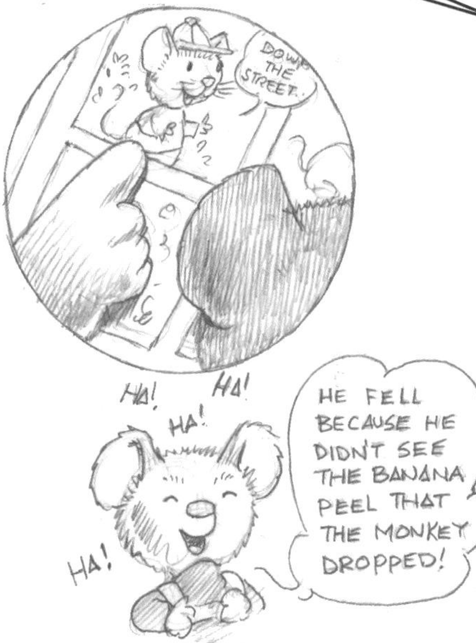
DOWN THE STREET.
HA! HA! HA! HA!
HE FELL BECAUSE HE DIDN'T SEE THE BANANA PEEL THAT THE MONKEY DROPPED!

4 LET THE PICTURES TELL THE STORY

In a comic, you can often read the story even if you don't know all the words. Encourage young readers to tell you what's happening based on the facial expressions and body language.

5 GET OUT THE CRAYONS

Kids see the hand of the author in a comic and it makes them want to tell their own stories. Encourage them to talk, write and draw!

Get kids talking, and you'll be surprised at how perceptive they are about pictures.

6 LET THEM GUESS

Comics provide a large amount of context for the words, so let young readers make informed guesses, and don't over-correct. In this panel, the artist shows a pirate ship, two pirate hats, and two pirate flags the first time the word "PIRATE" is introduced.

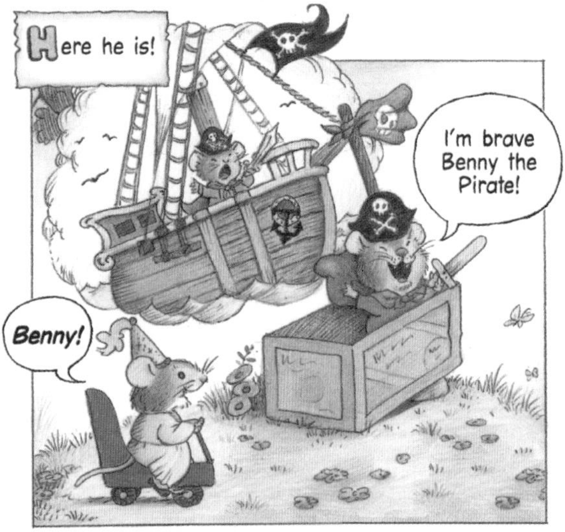
Here he is!
I'm brave Benny the Pirate!
Benny!

HOW TO "TOON INTO READING"

in a few simple steps:

Our goal is to get kids reading—and we know kids LOVE comics. We publish award-winning early readers in comics form for elementary and early middle school, and present them in three levels.

1 FIND THE RIGHT BOOK

Veteran teacher Cindy Rosado tells what makes a good book for beginning and struggling readers alike: "A vetted vocabulary, plenty of picture clues, repetition, and a clear and compelling story. Also, the book shouldn't be too easy—or the reader won't learn, but neither should it be too hard—or he or she may get discouraged."

The TOON INTO READING!™ program is designed for beginning readers and works wonders with reluctant readers.

MO AND JO
FIGHTING TOGETHER FOREVER
BENJAMIN BEAR
in Fuzzy Thinking
ZIG AND WIKKI
NADJA SPIEGELMAN & TRADE LOEFFLER
BENNY AND PENNY
THE BIG NO-NO!
Oh, Benny, this is a very big NO-NO!
Yes!
GEOFFREY HAYES
CHICK & CHICKIE
PLAY ALL DAY!
What do you want to play?
A TOON BOOK BY
Claude Ponti
Little Mouse
Gets Ready
THAT'S ME!
A TOON BOOK BY
Jeff Smith
THE SHARK KING

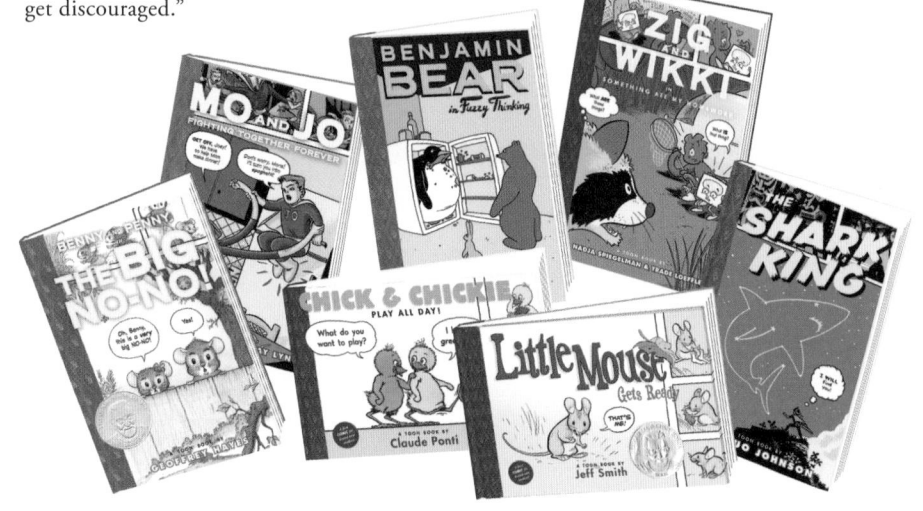

2 TAKE TIME WITH SILENT PANELS

Comics use panels to mark time, and silent panels count. Look and "read" even when there are no words. Often, humor is all in the timing!

KNOCK! KNOCK!
TRICK OR TREAT!

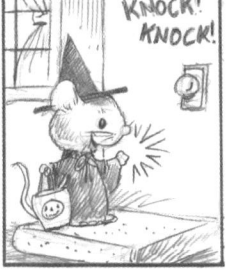

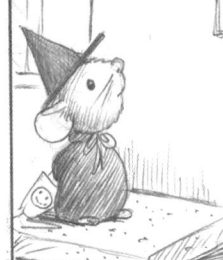

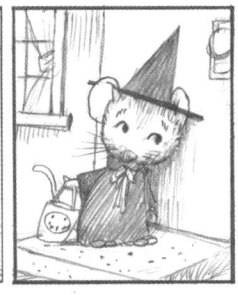

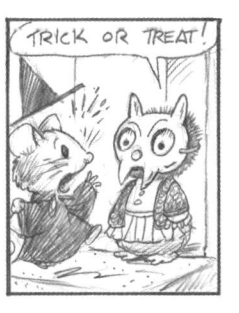